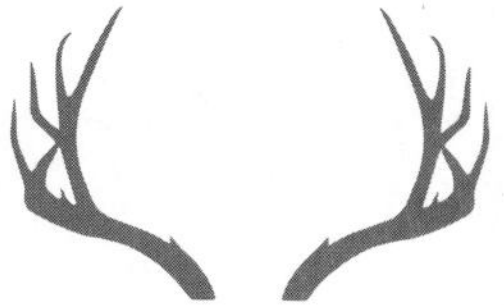

Presented to ______________________________

By ______________________________

On the Occasion of ______________________________

____

Date ______________________________

HUNT OF A LIFETIME

An Outdoorsman's Journey to Prayer

by

SCOTT B. LEMASTERS

Terre Haute, Indiana

PrayerShop Publishing is the publishing arm of the Church Prayer Leaders Network.

The Church Prayer Leaders Network exists to equip and inspire local churches and their prayer leaders in their desire to disciple their people in prayer and to become a "house of prayer for all nations." Its online store, prayershop.org, has more than 150 prayer resources available for purchase or download.

ISBN (Print): 978-1-935012-93-1
ISBN (E-Book): 978-1-935012-94-8

Cover photo by Charles J. Alsheimer

Original Edit by Kimberly Shumate, ReVision Editing Agency

Final Edit: David Fessenden

1 2 3 4 5 | 2020 2021 2022 2023 2024

Dedication and Acknowledgments

To Cat, Sarah, and Eli: I love each of you with all of my heart, and I thank God for His grace and overwhelming blessings on our family.

To Steve Chapman, Kimberly Shumate, and Jon Graf: Thank you for your generous support and encouragement. Praise God for leading me to you.

CONTENTS

FOREWORD

By Steve Chapman

I was introduced to Scott B. Lemasters' writing through a story sent to me about his goat hunt in the mountains of Southeast Alaska. My response to his narrative of the experience was the highest compliment I could offer—I wrote back, "I can tell that you've actually been there." I do not often react that way to wilderness stories, but Scott's description stirred something familiar in me as an outdoorsman—the kind of feeling that feeds my passion for the wild.

Having captured my attention with his writing, I was glad to get the manuscript for his book titled, *Hunt of a Lifetime: An Outdoorsman's Journey to Prayer.* I discovered as I read through the chapters that there's a purpose for it that goes beyond enjoyable familiar imagery.

Perhaps the best way to describe the book is to use a reference to the movie *Jeremiah Johnson.* Jeremiah left civilization in the city to go it alone into the mountain wilderness. At a time in his wandering when he needed a friend the most, he encountered an older man named "Bear Claw." Drawing from his own experience as a survivor in the untamed wilderness, Bear Claw helped the young wanderer learn more about how to navigate the roughness and dangers of the remote mountains.

Scott's book can be a timely "Bear Claw" encounter for the "Jeremiah Johnsons" who are on the journey to heaven through the wilderness of this world. Reading it can help guide the heart to life-changing spiritual insights. Some are revealed through the accounts of timeless biblical characters who were outdoor types, and some come from Scott's personal collection of experiences as an outdoorsman.

Your journey will be blessed by this book.

Steve Chapman
Author, *A Look at Life from a Deer Stand*

INTRODUCTION

The Lord will guide you always . . . —Isaiah 58:11

As I sat down at my kitchen counter and began to write this book in 2016, I felt I had very little choice in the matter. For nearly twenty years, the Lord has put a few special Scripture passages on my heart, revealing their meaning, and shaping me—through my missteps and failures—until I felt compelled to "stretch out" my hand (Matthew 12:13) to start to type, praying that the words would come. And like all Christians, my walk with the Lord is not yet complete, but I continue to pray and try to wait, listen, understand, and take to heart what I hear Him telling me. This book is the result of years of preparation within the journey.

I don't share these details with you to lift up myself. It's quite the opposite. As a "hands on" type of guy, I've struggled to learn from the wisdom and advice of others. For many years, I only involved God in the parts of my life where I needed Him or wanted Him to be. I think many men tend to struggle with this. But my failures to fully listen and learn from God and others come from my strong desire to be in control. This disposition has led me to make a lot of mistakes—blessed mistakes. Blessed, because God has used them—and the frustration, grief, and pain attached to them—to shape me into the man I am today. Please understand; I'm not at all proud of these mistakes, but I share them with you in the same way Kris Kristofferson intended when he wrote the lyrics to his song, "Why Me."

> Try me, Lord, if you think there's a way
> I can try to repay all I've taken from you.
> Maybe, Lord, I can show someone else
> What I've been through myself
> on my way back to you.[1]

Perhaps like me, you're a passionate hunter and fisherman. I grew up fishing for bass, crappie, and muskie with my father, and still do.

Together, we've enjoyed fishing all over the world—from tiger fish on the Zambezi River, to red salmon on Kodiak Island, to walleye on the Great Lakes. I've also been blessed to pursue a wide variety of big-game animals from do-it-yourself hunts for Dall sheep, coastal brown bear, moose, and whitetail deer, to guided hunts for Cape buffalo, sable, mule deer, and mountain lion.

While I've always felt a greater sense of satisfaction on the unguided trips—there's that control thing again—even my best do-it-yourself hunts were successful because I listened to and learned from what others were willing to share with me. And sometimes, we simply *must* be guided to reach a higher ground of knowledge than we could ever find on our own.

I think you know where I'm going with this. After wasting so many years as a believer not allowing God to be my Guide, I failed to grow spiritually or gain the wisdom and momentum that He longed for me to have. Through my stubbornness, I also missed opportunities to serve Him. Sadly, even when He brought me significant insights through my failures, I consciously and unconsciously refused to grant Him entry into many other aspects of my journey.

I first experienced God's saving grace at the age of twenty-six, yet through to my late-forties, I still only granted Him access in certain areas of my life by "invitation only." I opened to Him only select portions of my finances, career, marriage, children, and friendships—sparingly and self-managed. As a result, my relationship with the Lord suffered. And as Oswald Chambers put it so perfectly, "If I allow any private deflection from God in my life, everyone about me suffers."[2]

But there's good news in the midst of this suffering for you and me. We are blessed with a Lord and Savior who loves each of us deeply and personally. He cares for you and knows everything about you. More importantly, He wants an intimate relationship with you and longs for you to rest entirely in Him and experience His love and peace. And to bring you this peace—peace that overcomes your struggles, shame, hurts, anxieties or addictions—He lovingly took on our human form.

Born to a poor family that would settle in the rural town of Nazareth, Jesus lived the life in communion with the Father that you and I were created to live. And in the greatest act of personal sacrifice ever witnessed, He became our Savior. Forever balancing humankind's sin-filled ledger with God, He lovingly laid down His life on the cross. The Lamb of God, Jesus Christ, loves us so much that He sacrificed His life to free us forever from our sins. He traded His life—His holy and perfect life—to acquire our forgiveness from our God, the Father. And three days later, when He was resurrected on Easter morning, He defeated death and gave each of us the hope and promise of eternal life with Him. Death could not defeat Him, and He offers the same victory to you and me if we seek Him with all our heart, with all our soul, and with all our strength (Deuteronomy 6:5).

To fully grasp these matters in your own life, I challenge you to step out of your comfort zone into territories unexplored. From windswept mountain peaks to the darkest valleys of your past, God is calling to you. And I hope by reading this book, you will find your way to a quiet place of reflection and prayer amid the struggles and victories that you meet along the way.

As you allow the Lord to be your Guide—giving Him full access to all of the steep ravines and rocky terrain of a guarded heart—listen. When you bark at your children or spouse, feel the guilt of racking up credit card debt, search the internet for pornography, or gossip about others, listen. Do you hear God speaking or are you acknowledging Him only when and where it will benefit you? If so, you're missing out on His very best for you.

I'm not telling you this is going to be easy. I know it's not. But the first step is to ask God to help you give up all control to Him. He's pursuing you, even now. Take this opportunity to reach out to Him and simply let the Lord be your Guide. What an extraordinary adventure He has planned for you. And I hope that this book is the beginning of a lifelong journey that helps to form a deeper and lasting relationship with the Fisher of Men.

CHAPTER ONE

LISTEN AND HEAR THE CALL OF GOD

The God who made the world and everything in it is the Lord of heaven and earth and does not live in temples built by human hands. —Acts 17:24

In the fall of 2008, I woke early from my tent in the Wrangell Mountains of Alaska to check the weather and visibility. To my excitement, it was the first clear morning in three days. My companion Gary and I quickly loaded our packs. And while we were already camped above the alpine, we began to climb. Full of energy and anticipation, we soon found ourselves on a perch nearly 2,000 feet above our base camp, searching for a bachelor group of Dall sheep making the morning ascent from their evening grazing grounds.

Ewes and lambs were everywhere to be seen—white dots on distant ridges and mountainsides—but it was Gary that spotted the procession of ten rams winding their way upward. We followed them intently through our spotting scope until they came to rest on a ridgeline a couple of miles away and roughly 1,500 feet below us. What followed was one of the most joy-filled outdoor experiences of my life.

Quickly and quietly, Gary and I descended to a knoll above the rams. It was a cool morning with a light breeze in our faces, but the sun on our backs kept us warm. Far below us was the dry bed of an ancient glacier. The lichens, grasses, and shrubs were in a full fall display—reds, browns, yellows, and oranges surrounded us. There we rested on our stomachs and watched these beautiful, powerful, bright white sheep for nearly an hour, examining each one.

In that moment, creation itself truly spoke to me. Through "the concert pitch of nature around" us, I sensed the Creator's presence and yearned "for the truth in my heart."[3] Praise God for such beauty and the joy of nature He placed in our soul!

True outdoorsmen—that's men and women, mind you—are all inspired in this way by nature. We have a heartfelt connection to creation that is undeniable. And the stronger this pull, the more compelled we are to intertwine our pastimes, careers, homes, and families with it. As a follower of Christ, I believe our desire to commune with nature is driven by the powerful presence of God in His creation. This passionate bond we sense, whether we recognize it or not, is a call from God—an intuitive awareness of Him.

No matter where we are on our journey with the Lord, earnest prayer is essential (Colossians 4:2). Journaling is also a helpful tool during those times when we struggle to pray. It helps us sort through thoughts and emotions, and begin what I hope will be a lifelong conversation with the One who created us.

Whether you're a "new" Christian, a lifelong follower, or somewhere in between, we're all capable of spiritual apathy—a state of disengagement in our spiritual lives. During one of my own periods of spiritual indifference, I discovered that by recording my thoughts and prayers on paper, I was able to re-energize my spiritual awareness. Now, I hardly go a day without it.

The first time I remember experiencing joy, I was eight years old and fishing with my father. It had such a profound impact on me that I can recall it now forty years later. But, there were other moments that are now lost to me—encounters that were worthy of recording and quietly contemplating. These days, I keep a notebook in my pack and tackle box because I never know when to expect them.

Now think back to the first time that you felt the healing grace of God. Can you picture it, feel it, sense His omnipotence within? If not, is it due to your refusal to allow Him full access to and involvement in every part of your life? Are you now ready and willing to give up all control to Him?

Please know that I don't raise these questions to judge you, but quite the opposite. These are key steps that confront every Christian as they grow in their faith. They take time, and we should be patient with ourselves and "keep asking that the God of our Lord Jesus Christ" give us "the Spirit of wisdom and revelation, so that" we "may know Him better" (Ephesians 1:17).

I truly hope that you will seek more opportunities to get alone with Christ. Finding quiet time to talk with Him daily is the most precious time of all, and we don't have to be in the wild to do it. Yes, I wish that I could get alone with Him in my favorite outdoor destination every day, but all you really need to do is "go into your room, close the door, and pray to your Father" (Matthew 6:6).

This solitude with Christ not only reflects the personal time and communication every deep and lasting relationship requires, but gives us the strength each day to live a Christ-conscious life. Or as Henri Nouwen offered in *Making All Things New*, "Without solitude it is virtually impossible to live a spiritual life. Solitude begins with a time and place for God, and Him alone. If we really believe not only that God exists, but also that He is actively present in our lives—healing, teaching, and *guiding*—we need to set aside a time and space to give Him our undivided attention."[4]

I ask you now to take the time to reflect and answer the following questions so that you, too, can strengthen your relationship with God.

Questions for reflection and meditation:

1. What are your favorite outdoor activities, and what is it about these activities that you enjoy?
2. What people are involved?
3. Who among these folks do you share a sense of fellowship?
4. Where is your favorite outdoor destination, and why? If there's an emotional connection, describe it.
5. Briefly describe a favorite moment where you enjoyed quiet time alone in nature. What was it about the moment that made it special?
6. Have you ever experienced moments where you sensed God's presence in nature or elsewhere? If so, briefly describe one

of them. Who was present, what was the location, and what did you feel?

Prayer:

Lord Jesus, as I sit quietly alone with You and reflect on my connection to Your creation, I give thanks. Thank You for the beauty and wonder that stirs my spirit. Thank You for the fellowship I sense with my closest friends and family when we enjoy the outdoors, even the simplest campfire. And thank You for the passion You placed in my heart that continues to draw me to the field and mountain and forest. I acknowledge today, Father, that there's more to these emotions than simple happiness. You placed this desire, this attachment to nature deep within my soul. It's a place where we meet and connect—You and me. And it's an opportunity to grow closer to You, if only I would engage You in conversation.

So, let's talk, Lord. I'm going to need Your help. Open my heart to Your Word. Enable me to sense Your presence as I share with You my hopes, pains and desires. Help me to hear Your gentle whisper, and stir my soul in such a way that it demands time alone with You each day in prayer.

CHAPTER TWO

WALK THE DOCKS WITH THE FISHER OF MEN

"Come, follow me," Jesus said, "and I will make you fishers of men." —Matthew 4:19

As a boy, I vividly remember riding my bike to the small marina near our home on the Chesapeake Bay. Depending on the time of year, I eagerly anticipated the fishermen's catch— bushels of crab, fish, or oysters—and enjoyed watching them offload it at the dock. These were strong, rugged men, often red-faced from the sun, wind, or cold. Their hands were heavily calloused. They and their boats had proven themselves able in the roughest conditions. Yet, despite their tough outward appearance, these men were genuinely friendly, proud of their profession, and eager to share and talk with me as I walked the docks around the marina.

When I grew older and joined the Coast Guard, I got to know commercial fishermen in the North Atlantic, Gulf of Mexico, Southeast Alaska, and Bering Sea. In time, I came to recognize that these men shared many qualities with the fishermen I knew back home. They were independent and self-employed; men who had to work with their hands and their minds to be successful. It seemed to come so natural to them.

They were critical thinkers, capable of giving tough criticism if it was deserved. They weren't easily impressed, and even if they didn't have a relationship with God, they possessed a love, respect, and fear for the wonder, beauty, and power of nature. Whether they knew it or not, God reached out to them through the majesty of His creation, and they responded by choosing a profession that allowed them to spend their lives outdoors.

These insights led me to draw comfort from the fact that Jesus called four fishermen to be His disciples. He could have selected religious leaders and other people of greater status from the community. Instead, the first four men He sought were commercial fishermen from the Sea of Galilee. The more I contemplated the similarities modern fishermen share with one another, the more it shaped how I viewed the four fishermen disciples. Think about it—Simon, Andrew, James, and John couldn't have been all that different. You can hear it in the nicknames that Jesus gave them, referring to Simon Peter as the "Rock" (Matthew 6:18) and James and John as the "Sons of Thunder" (Mark 3:17). Andrew, a follower of John the Baptist, ". . . was the means of igniting his brother Peter, when he brought him to Jesus."[5]

These were men of strong conviction who went on to become key leaders in the early church. They were true outdoorsmen; men that chose to make their living on the water. As sons of fishermen, they must have had a healthy respect for the power of the sea, yet were thankful for its bounty. As an avid outdoorsman, I feel a great sense of connection with these men, and I believe they shared my love of nature and felt the joy that it brings.

Yet, knowing everything we know about them, it can still be intimidating to put yourself in their place. How inspiring was Christ that day by the Sea of Galilee to offer His invitation? Peter and Andrew "at once left their nets and followed Him" (Matthew 4:20). James and John "were in a boat with their father Zebedee, preparing their nets… and immediately they left the boat and their father and followed Him" (Matthew 4:21–22). It makes me wonder how the tough, opinionated fishermen I walked the docks with in Alaska and Virginia would have responded to His call. What would we do?

I want to believe that I would have followed Him that day. That the awe-inspiring nature of being in the presence of Christ would leave me no choice. Or, would I have been more like the Pharisees and Sadducees and denied Him? After all, I spent the majority of my adult life willing to acknowledge Christ's existence and thankful for His saving grace, but I was unwilling to give up control to Him. Would I have let Christ be my Guide when He said, "Come, follow me" (Matthew 4:19)?

The following questions may help to provide the answers to the difficult scenarios in your faith walk.

Questions for reflection and meditation:

1. What activities and interests from your childhood still appeal to you today?
2. Which people involved in these childhood activities influenced you most?
3. How did they influence you, and what did you learn from them?
4. Aside from Christ, what people in the Bible do you identify with the most?
5. Why do you sense this connection—what is it about them or their circumstances?
6. In what ways do these people from your past and those you identify with in the Bible give you hope?

Prayer:

Father, as I reflect on the disciples' willingness to, literally, drop everything and follow You, I feel a touch of self-doubt come over me. Their resolute courage, their desire to know You more overruled every other aspect of their lives. I struggle to see myself doing the same at Your call. After all, I spent much of my life denying You access to parts of me that I fought to control, wanting to lead and not follow.

So, as I sit here and reflect on these men—fishermen that shared my passion for Your creation—I find hope in identifying with them. They did not know that You were the Son of God when they dropped their nets and walked away from all they knew and loved. But they did sense the great hope that you offered and yearned to know more. And I can so relate to that—a deep yearning, a sense that there's more to be explored and know about You and Your way.

Please grant me courage, Lord Jesus—the kind of courage to let go of everything and follow You. Deep within me, I know that it is my life's greatest journey. It's so incredibly difficult, Father. Help me to take this bold step—not just today, but every day—and follow You.

CHAPTER THREE

TRACK YOUR JOY TO HIS GRACE

Let the sea resound, and everything in it, the world and all who live in it. Let the rivers clap their hands, let the mountains sing together for joy. —Psalm 98:7, 8

My emotions and soul are stirred by nature. Like many of you, it led me to pursue hobbies and a career, even a honeymoon, that would allow me to maximize the time spent outdoors. My earliest recollection of these longings was as an eight-year-old, fishing with my father and a close friend on an old mill pond near our home. Unlike most of our fishing trips, we took a break for lunch that day, beached the boat, and fried up some of the fish we caught. My dad and I had many adventures together, but this was something new and exciting.

It was a beautiful, crisp fall day, and the fish tasted better than it ever had before. But beyond just the fun we were having, there was something else about that shore lunch—something about the fellowship, the outdoors, and the food—that left me feeling more than simple pleasure. I felt joy!

Since that time, I've experienced that same joy during quiet walks alone in the woods, around campfires with close friends, and during those unexpected "snapshots" of beauty we occasionally encounter in God's world. In time, I began to refer to these experiences as "shore lunch moments" in memory of that meal on the beach with my dad because they always involved some combination of nature, fellowship, and a strong sense of God's presence or a prayer fulfilled.

It's so important to remember that there's a difference between pleasure and joy. The pleasure you get from catching a fish or camping with your family is not joy. It may be fun, recreational, relaxing, and satisfying, but it isn't joy. Joy goes much deeper. As C.S. Lewis points out in his book *Surprised by Joy*, joy isn't something that can be pursued like a fish or ascended like a mountain. It is an unanticipated "by-product" of something else.[6] To attempt to manufacture joy is futile.

As strange as it sounds, I have never experienced joy while concentrating on my feelings. Self-centeredness or thinking inwardly about personal matters suffocates my joy. My joy-filled moments have always resulted from outward contemplation of natural beauty, prayer, or enjoying fellowship with close friends. The stuff that life is made of.

Now consider this: If you occasionally experience joy in God's creation—through His calling out to you—how much greater and more complete will your joy be when you respond? For many years I failed to return His calls. I wasn't able to relinquish control to Him. I ignored the stabbing of pain of sin in order to maintain my "freedom." The irony is unsettling, even now.

It is only when we dedicate ourselves to Him that we begin to experience the full peace and joy of God. This is only possible through the grace of God. You are on the track—on the track of such grace—when you experience those moments of joy in nature. But to truly pursue it, you must return His call and follow Him. That's how it starts—calling out to Him in prayer.

It is a life dedicated to Him, a Christ-centered obedient life, that experiences joy on a grander scale—a component of the "fruit of the Spirit" (Galatians 5:22). But it is only available to us through the grace of God. It originates from the true freedom we experience when we pursue God with our whole heart. Such grace and joy and peace go well beyond the moments of joy we experience in nature because it requires so much more of us. It's the difference between hearing God's call and responding to it.

Perhaps the purest description of this joy is provided by Brother Lawrence in *The Practice of the Presence of God.* As a poor man working in the kitchen of a seventeenth-century monastery, Lawrence said, “There is no sweeter manner of living in the world than continuous communion with God. Only those who have experienced it can understand.”[7] Living in absolute poverty, Lawrence experienced the kind of joy-filled life that Paul contemplated when he wrote, “Whatever you do, do it all for the glory of God” (1 Corinthians 10:31).

Brother Lawrence also understood that maintaining this moment-by-moment relationship with God was extremely challenging and required deep commitment. It was his lifelong passion. Through his experiences he came to learn that life’s dull and mundane activities are often the most difficult times to stay focused on Jesus. His wisdom and clarity brought many people—from bishops to fellow lay members—to Brother Lawrence for spiritual guidance.

He shared with them his love of the Lord and reminded them to “not be discouraged by the resistance you will encounter from your human nature; you must go against your human inclinations. Often, in the beginning, you will think that you are wasting time, but you must go on, be determined and persevere in it until death, despite all the difficulties.”[8] This is a powerful message for anyone seeking to establish or deepen their relationship with Christ. And it can only be accomplished if you are willing to “let go and cling to God with everything that’s in you.”[9]

Oswald Chambers wrote in *My Utmost for His Highest* that “Some people do a certain thing and the way in which they do it [makes holy] that thing forever afterwards. It may be the most commonplace thing, but after we have seen them do it, it becomes different.”[10] That was definitely the case for those who were impacted by Lawrence’s Christ-centered approach to washing dishes, cleaning, and cooking. After his death, the Archbishop of Paris assembled and published Lawrence’s conversations. As for Lawrence, he would die in “relative obscurity and pain and perfect joy.”[11]

Take a moment to reflect and answer the following questions as honestly as you can.

Questions for reflection and meditation:

1. Think for a while and identify a joy-filled moment in your life—in nature or elsewhere—that stands out above the rest? Reflect and describe the circumstances that led to it.
2. Did you sense God's presence?
3. What "elements" were involved—fellowship with others, nature's beauty, etc.?
4. Has it changed you in any way going forward? If so, how?
5. If you are a Christian, describe the last time your relationship with Christ brought you joy?
6. If you aren't a follower of Christ, but are seeking God, please write a prayer telling Jesus you want a relationship with Him. Ask for His help with your struggles. Include questions that you would like Him to answer.
7. What are the steps you can take today to strengthen your relationship with God?

Prayer:

Lord Jesus, I come to You today with a heart full of God-given, joy-filled memories in the wild. Unspoken moments in the boat with my Dad, shared joy as one of my children catches a fish, fellowship with my closest friends around a campfire, and walks alone with You through familiar woods—such blessings! Yet, for much of my life, I left You there in the field. I returned to the "real world," resumed old patterns, and did not welcome You fully into my work, my family, or the relationships I pursued.

Father, please help me. I can't do this without You. I "stand on the mountain before" You (1 Kings 19:11) today and ask You to stir my soul with an overwhelming awareness of Your presence no matter the scene or activity—on my drive to work, when I'm hurt by a close friend or loved one, at a ball game, or watching television. It doesn't matter. All I know is that I don't want to move any further forward without You leading me.

This will take time and effort and commitment on my part, Lord. I understand. Guide me, rebuke me, whisper to me Your direction. And please place on my heart the loving burden to seek Your will in every aspect of my life.

CHAPTER FOUR

SET YOUR ANCHOR ON HIM

We have this hope as an anchor for the soul, firm and secure. —Hebrews 6:19

I am blessed to share my emotional connection to nature with my father. We've had many outdoor adventures together, but few days have surpassed March 4, 2004 on the old, seventy-five-acre mill pond near our home. The days and the water had begun to warm. We hoped to catch the bass gorging themselves on shad before the spring spawn.

It was overcast and drizzly as we loaded our gear into our twelve-foot Sears Gamefisher. The conditions were perfect for fishing the shallows where we hoped the shad would be. By 10 a.m. we had already boated a couple five-pounders and several more "chunks." My dad, who quite truly fished this pond a thousand times, commented that he'd never experienced a morning like this one. It was only a few minutes later that I boated a ten-pounder, the largest bass either of us had ever caught.

After the shock and shakes wore off a bit, there was some good-natured crowing coming from the bow of the boat where I sat. You see, it's a rare day when I outdo my dad at fishing. Then, around 1 P.M., he caught an eight-pounder, the second largest fish we'd ever caught on this pond. I began to let up a bit, but dad's intensity remained. He realized more than I did at the time what a rare day this was and fished with even greater focus than usual.

Then it happened. When I saw the spine of the fish pulling away from the boat, I knew it was the biggest fish either of us had seen all day. I reached for the net as Dad adjusted his drag. Once boated, my reign as the family's biggest bass-catcher was over. It lasted for only six hours. Dad's bass was twelve pounds, two ounces. And then the crowing began from the stern of the boat!

Now, I'm blessed to share my faith with my father. One of our favorite quotes from Oswald Chambers is, "Faith is the heroic effort of your life; fling yourself in reckless confidence on God . . . the real meaning of eternal life is a life that can face anything it has to without wavering. If we take this view, life becomes one great romance, a glorious opportunity for seeing marvelous things all the time."

That day of fishing on the mill pond was, obviously, a marvelous father-son experience. But there are also marvelous opportunities in the smallest moments and even in our tragedies, if we know Christ. As Richard Fuller offered, "Anchor yourself steadfastly on the Lord. And then, come what may."[12] Of course, this quote begs the question: Where have you set your anchor?

When our anchor isn't set on God, we toss about on the open water. We are vulnerable to life's turbulent currents and winds. One such account is documented in the book *Surprised By Joy*. Like you, perhaps, there was a period in C.S. Lewis's life when he desperately pursued joy only to chase it away by his "greedy impatience to snare it."[13] At that time, Lewis was an atheist, but he was desperately searching for answers. He described his desperation as growing to the point where all that he believed to be real was "grim and meaningless" with the exception of "certain people and nature herself."[14] Ultimately, like many of us with this powerful connection to God's creation, fellowship, and "the call" he sensed in nature, helped lead Lewis to Christ.

Of course, every Christian's story of that moment where they accept Christ as their Savior is different, but there are a few common threads worth mentioning. First, most or all of us experience an intuitive yearning—a sense that something is missing or reaching out to us. Many people try to fill this void with worldly things and activities in the same way people often errantly pursue and substitute sex when they are seeking love. Indebtedness, alcoholism, and obsession are common on the long list of the problems that stem from our misguided attempts to satisfy the yearning in our soul with earthly idols rather than the Holy Spirit.

Next, there must be a response—a willingness to actively seek God through prayer, Bible study, and fellowship with Christians. It is something many refer to as "answering God's call." Or, as Oswald Chambers put it, "We have to take the first step as though there were no God . . . do the thing and not lie like a log."[15] It is at this point, when you begin to regularly pray in response to God's call, that your dialogue with Him begins. In your prayers, journaling, fellowship, and day-to-day activities, you get a very real sense that He is conversing with you. He puts circumstances and people in your life to answer your questions and bring you to a deeper understanding of what it means to have a relationship with Him.

Finally, we reach that moment of heartfelt understanding of the sacrifice Jesus made for us. The betrayal by His closest friends; the humiliation of Christ as He was accused and sentenced; and the agonizing death that followed. We understand the power in the blood He shed on the cross—that God does not forgive us out of sympathy, but Christ's death on the cross and His resurrection was the only way to set things right for all of mankind across all of time. And we understand that it has already been done for us. All that we need to do is accept His forgiveness and follow Him.

This supernatural insight comes with deep emotional stirrings of gratitude and love and shame—shame that He had to die to account for our sins and willfulness. You may have been through a very painful experience to arrive at this point, and the wave of emotions that hits you can be overwhelming. The circumstances and pain that lead us to Christ are often among the most difficult periods of our lives. In time, though, we learn and trust that "In all things, God works for the good of those who love Him" (Romans 8:28).

My moment occurred while sitting across the table from my grandfather in a small diner in Ohio. He was a Nazarene minister, full of hellfire and brimstone from bygone days. I had a deep love, respect, and fear for the man. He was stern and rigid in his convictions. Our strong and sometimes overbearing personalities were very similar, and while he wasn't always a very good listener, I always felt that we understood each other.

And so, at the age of twenty-six, I found myself across the table from him struggling to tell him that I wanted to divorce my wife. In the days leading up to this breakfast, I grew more and more afraid of his judgment, and also how I would respond to it. But as the words stumbled out of my mouth and my apprehension peaked, he looked at me lovingly and simply said, "Scott, you know that God forgives you, don't you?"

Well, there it was. It took my grandfather—a man I feared perhaps more than God—to help me really understand the truth and significance of Christ's redeeming grace. I'd spent many weeks leading up to that moment praying to God, crying for direction, and now, I had my answer. An answer that revealed the true power of God's forgiving nature.

A powerful story of how God's light reached two unbelievers is detailed in Sheldon Vanauken's *A Severe Mercy*. Similar to C.S. Lewis, Sheldon and his wife were atheists with a profound love of nature. And, while they were not fully aware, God called out to them one joy-filled evening on their sailboat, *The Grey Goose*.

> The air was cool and fresh. Ten thousand brilliant stars arched across the sky. But what transfixed us was phosphorescence. Every little wave rolling into the cove was crested with cold fire. The anchor rode was a line of fire going down into the depths, and fish moving about left trails of fire. The night of the sea-fire . . . Neither of us spoke, not so much as whispered a word. We were together, we were close, we were overwhelmed by a great beauty. All about us was the extraordinary beauty of the sea-fire and the glittering stars overhead. We were full of wonder—and joy.[16]

While Sheldon and his wife sensed and ultimately responded to God's call through fellowship and study, their experiences were very different. More driven by her sense of feeling, Sheldon's wife was the first to realize that her husband's love was not enough to sustain her. Persuaded more by her emotional connection to God and a keen awareness of His forgiving nature, she made the "leap"[17] before Sheldon was ready.

This became a rub in their relationship. Sheldon was very aware that God was now first in her life, ahead of himself. Still, he dutifully continued in his biblical studies and fellowship with other Christians in response to the call. He searched for pieces of information that would prove God's existence and make Christ's resurrection irrefutable. He studied. He read. He wanted proof. His scholarly pursuit of God grew until one day he recognized emotionally that he could no longer imagine a life without God in it. There was no going back. He finally believed. He had come to the inescapable truth revealed in Galatians 4:9: "Now that you have come to know God—or rather are known by God—how is it that you are turning back?"

All of these stories that I've shared of C.S. Lewis, myself, and the Vanaukens illustrate that we all felt a yearning, a call heard through God's creation. We responded to this call by reaching out to Him in prayer, study, and fellowship. That is all it takes to get the conversation started with God. If you will earnestly and diligently reach out to God with a desire to know Him better, He will respond. It's promised: "Come near to God and He will come near to you" (James 4:8). If you follow through, I'm confident that, in time, you will come to a deeper understanding of the supreme sacrifice Christ made for us.

For many years, I was satisfied to enjoy the short-lived thrills I experienced outdoors, or to put it another way, I turned nature into my religion until it was no longer enough to sustain me. It was only after I began to earnestly seek God and "set my anchor" on Him that the answers began to come. This leads us to a difficult question in any faith journey, but it is unavoidable: Where is your anchor set—your job, your finances, your family? Without God as your Lord and Savior, it is all meaningless. There's only one way to satisfy that yearning that you can't explain.

If you begin the conversation with God, seeking Him in prayer and listening for His voice, He will respond to you. He will bring people into your life seemingly out of nowhere to share their experiences and inspire you to move forward. Reach out to Him. Allow this journey to lead you to the power of His forgiveness and the saving grace which was achieved for you through the loving sacrifice and resurrection of Jesus Christ. It is a humbling experience to finally realize that He's been there all along, calling out to you. All you need do is anchor yourself steadfastly on Him.

I hope these questions will help you to reflect, pray, and answer God's call in your life.

Questions for reflection and meditation:

1. Recall a moment where you felt God's call in nature.
2. How did you respond to this call or feeling?
3. What else, if anything, could you have done to respond to God in this particular moment that would have deepened your relationship with Him?
4. If you can't think of a moment, can you remember an instance where you did something you knew to be wrong?
5. Did you feel guilt, sorrow, or distress?
6. Again, how could you have responded to God and grown closer to Him through this experience?

Prayer:

Father God, thank You for the yearning, the sense of "something more" you placed deep within my soul. I spent much of my life spiritually adrift. Refusing to give up control to You, I willfully chose to paddle wildly against life's currents. Too often, my loved ones, who were in the boat with me, also suffered. But today, with the clear-eyed wisdom that only You can give, I choose to set my anchor on You.

Holy Spirit, Your call is undeniable and persistent. It grows in strength as I respond with prayer. And as our conversation builds, I'm increasingly aware of the people and circumstances You bring to me. With every new day, please grant me greater knowledge of You and Your will for my life. Give me a love for You that burns with understanding. Help me to nurture the faith, trust, and patience necessary to follow and rest in You. There is no other pathway or course to peace.

CHAPTER FIVE

REST IN THE HANDS OF THE HEAVENLY ARCHER

But his bow remained steady, his strong arms stayed limber, because of the hand of the Mighty One of Jacob, because of the Shepherd, the Rock of Israel.
—Genesis 49:24

In December of 2016, my dad and I sat in a small ground blind on a farm near Adrian, Michigan. It was a cold, still morning with a few inches of snow on the ground. A layer of ice had formed on the surface of the snow after a hard night's freeze. And the bright white canvas that surrounded us was ideal for spotting game. We heard and saw the deer approaching long before I needed to raise my bow.

My heart raced and my mind reflected as we huddled and waited for the deer to arrive. How blessed I was to share this moment with my father! The quiet fellowship of a father and son is a precious gift from God. I am blessed with a dad that has seen me through some incredibly difficult times. In truth, his love and grace has shaped how I view our Father. After all, "If you, then, though you are evil, know how to give good gifts to your children, how much more will your Father in heaven give good gifts to those who ask him!" (Matthew 7:11). This experience has led me to rest in Him more, to understand that we are blessed with a Savior in Jesus Christ that will guide and comfort us through the valley of the shadow of death (see Psalm 23:4).

For you bow hunters, Oswald Chambers wrote in *My Utmost for His Highest* that our "life is in the hands of God like a bow and arrow is in the hands of an archer. God is aiming at something [that we] cannot see, and He stretches and strains [us] till His purpose is in sight, then He lets us fly. Trust yourself in God's hands."[18]

Of course, this degree of trust requires deep faith in God—the kind of faith that must be nurtured and grown over time. It's the kind of faith that only matures as we learn to seek God first and strive to abide in Him throughout our day. Whether you refer to God as your Guide or heavenly Archer, the analogy, the question, is the same. Do you want Him (have you asked Him) to be your Guide?

For many years, even after I came to know Christ following the encounter with my grandfather, I stubbornly refused to surrender control. I knowingly prevented Him from entering key areas of my life—finances, relationships, work. I denied the need for His presence. Even worse, I called upon Him only when it benefited me.

We can all agree that there are days when we could all use a miracle, and God wants us to come to Him in prayer about our needs and wants. But this can't be the primary focus of our relationship with Him. If Christ is truly our Guide, we need to focus on Him. It's like any relationship in our lives—when we focus only on what we want from the other person, it's not healthy or rewarding. That's exactly what happened to the nation of Israel.

In spite of the many miraculous events that led the Jewish nation out of Egypt and sustained them in the desert, they continued to doubt God and think only of themselves. They doubted Him to the point where they wished they had remained in Egypt as slaves (see Numbers 11:20). That's an incredible thought. Due to their willful disobedience, an entire generation was forbidden from entering the land "flowing with milk and honey" (Deuteronomy 26:9). Sadly, their children suffered this "disinheritance" along with them in the desert for 40 years. Talk about a dry spell!

My family and I have certainly suffered from my "desert experiences." For many years, I stayed so late at work that I neglected my wife and children. I justified it with the worldly notion that it was necessary in order to provide for them. To some extent, it was. But at some point, I chose to work later to satisfy my own competitive nature and desire for achievement. I was often rewarded for this behavior, further justifying it in my mind. But all along, I dealt with deep feelings of unhappiness and regret that often it inflicted pain upon my family, even when I was with them. I was not a joyful person. I found myself praying to God for help to be more patient and loving with my family, but I was unwilling to give up the control to Him.

Though you may be stuck in a similar place right now, we're all very different. Each of us is uniquely crafted by our heavenly Father. Some are perfectly able to work long hours and maintain healthy relationships with God and family, but may struggle in other areas. Excessive eating, sexual immorality, indebtedness, and gossiping keep them from calling upon God for help or give Him the final say in their lives. In their failure to do this, they end up hurting the ones they love the most.

Here's the question I want you to seriously consider: *If you're feeling pain and regret because of your choices, what are you doing about it?*

For years, I blamed the demands of my job for my problems and refused to acknowledge that it was my choice. When I finally reached the point where I could no longer stand the pain and I gave full control to God, I slowly and steadily began to find peace and happiness in the hands of the heavenly Archer. This isn't to say that I immediately ceased bad habits and sinful behavior—far from it. But in my heart, I gave up control to Him and acknowledged my need to seek His direction in every aspect of my life. And though I continue to make mistakes along the way, I try—through daily prayer and reflection—to listen, wait, understand, and accept what He is telling me.

As this conversation with God continues to grow, so does my awareness of His presence each and every day. I've begun to occasionally experience His joy during the most mundane and routine daily duties—that fruit of the Spirit experienced by Brother Lawrence. As I've taken time to reflect, that same Spirit convicts me for ignoring His obvious desire to be an active player in my life. I also feel extreme gratitude for His patience and forgiveness. What an extraordinary gift to receive!

Despite our broken nature, God continues to work on us every minute of every day. It's a never-ending restoration project, but one He takes great pride in—just as I do, and as you should.

As God perpetually works to refine us, we will begin to listen and improve certain behaviors as He reveals and addresses them. Yes, even the tough ones, such as cussing and careless words; surrendering to physical conditions and letting them dictate our mood; allowing weariness to affect our prayer life; neglecting our relationship with our children; judging or talking badly about others; and not exercising self-control.

We strive to overcome these deficiencies with varying degrees of success, but don't be discouraged (see Joshua 1:9). Continue to acknowledge them, and pray every day that God helps you turn over "everything in joyful trust" to Him.[19]

His faithful Archer's hand is upon you.

Questions for reflection and meditation:

1. Are there areas of your life where you are refusing to let Christ guide you? Write a list and track your improvement as God leads you to higher ground.
2. Do you feel a deep sense of regret and pain due to this behavior?
3. Are you hurting those closest to you in the process? If so, who?
4. What are you willing to do about it?
5. Put it in writing—creating a contract—and sign it. God is faithful to keep His end of the deal.

Prayer:

I come to You today, Jesus, asking You to knock over a few walls for me. They are barriers I've constructed in my mind in a misguided effort to retain control and deny access to You. You know them better than I. And You know that I'll probably start construction on a new wall or two as soon as these are destroyed. It's my nature. I am a master builder when it comes to my desire for control.

Please help me to rest in Your will, Lord. Help me to seek Your direction in every aspect of my life, to take the time to discuss the way forward with You before reacting emotionally or charging ahead. This is new territory for me. I will continue to make mistakes. Thank You for Your grace and persistent efforts to place Your loving burden on my soul. Please do not let up. Consume me with a Spirit-led, heartfelt desire to fly true and arrive at Your intended target.

CHAPTER SIX

CAMPFIRE WITH CHRIST

When they landed, they saw a fire of burning coals there with fish on it, and some bread. . . . Jesus said to them, "Come and have breakfast.—John 21:9, 12

So many of my best and fondest memories have taken place at my family's mountain home in Elk Fork, West Virginia. My sense of connection to Elk Fork spans the two centuries my ancestors have lived there. From the foundation stones under the corner of our cabin (cut by my great-great-grandfather) to the cabin itself, my sense of fellowship with God, friends, and family runs deep there.

During the years of my childhood I watched my grandfather use teams of horses to drag poplar logs to the cabin location. He hewed each beam by hand while my grandmother planted teeming flower beds around the hollow. This is the place of my first successful deer hunt with my father and numerous extended-family Thanksgiving gatherings. It's where my closest friends and I re-unite each year around the fire pit. I remember the first time each of my children walked the Elk Fork property.

And as I sit quietly alone inside the warm cabin this morning and reflect with a small fire in the fireplace, I'm deeply moved by this chapter's Scripture passage. I'm also reminded of Oswald Chambers' uplifting description of it: "The glory of the resurrection descends into a breakfast on the seashore."[20] This scene helps me to personally identify with the disciples who followed Jesus, and draws me closer to Him, knowing that He would fix a "shore lunch" for His followers and eat with them around the campfire.

For me, the account paints a vivid portrait of their friendship, turns their passion into holy activity, and makes sense of my own enthusiasm for nature and fellowship. By looking at this passage from Peter's perspective, it also helps me to appreciate the lengths that God will go to forgive us and draw us closer to Him—over a campfire!

In Luke 5, Jesus guides Peter to catch so many fish that their nets begin to break. It marks the beginning of a three-year period for Peter where he would leave all he had and everyone he loved to follow his Friend and Savior. In that short time, he witnessed miracle after miracle as well as the transfiguration of Jesus in the presence of Moses and Elijah. He shared private conversations with Him; he watched Him walk on water and calm the storm. Later, he dealt with the confusion and torment of the crucifixion and carried the burden of disowning Jesus—the One he loved most in this world. It's tragic to think about what must have been going on in Peter's head and heart at the time he disowned his best Friend, unto death.

Taking all of this into account, I believe that Peter and the other disciples must have developed a close relationship, a brotherhood, with one another—the kind of bond and kinship people form when facing the most dangerous and emotionally difficult circumstances together. And it was at this traumatic point in John's Gospel that Peter declares to the group, "I'm going out to fish" (John 21:3). After all, what would a fisherman do to deal with this kind of stress, pain, and internal struggle to set things right? He would seek a beloved connection with the presence of God in nature. Yes, Peter was indeed a true outdoorsman. It was also the perfect opportunity to find a sense of normalcy with his fellow disciples on that boat. Guys hanging out together through a very tough time.

On the boat with Peter was Thomas, Nathaniel, James, John, and two other disciples—men who had experienced the same incredible journey and felt the same immeasurable loss and sadness. While they fished through the night and caught nothing, you can imagine the conversations these men shared, retelling stories, reflecting on the past three years, and talking about what each of them might do next. This was a time for laughter, tears, and hope.

As the sun rose that morning on the Sea of Galilee, a man was there on the shore waiting for them. He called out to them, and for the second time in Peter's life, he was guided to a large haul of fish. It was in that moment that Peter—the "Rock," the commercial fisherman, the leader among the disciples—recognized Jesus, jumped into the water, and swam to Him like an excited child.

When Peter reached the shore, he "saw a fire of burning coals there with fish on it, and some bread." I have no doubt that for Peter, that food had more flavor, provided more comfort, and was prepared with more compassion than any meal he had ever eaten. He was, after all, sharing a meal with the Bread of Life. I'm fairly sure that in those last earthly moments with Christ, Peter also struggled with the guilt of denying Jesus and the need to seek His forgiveness. That forgiveness would come after the meal.

Looking across at his friend, Jesus asked Peter a question that wounded him deeply: "Do you love me?" Peter replied, "You know all these things; you know that I love you" (John 21:17). In doing so, Christ freed Peter of his guilt, and at the same time commissioned him to feed His sheep. Peter would forever abandon himself to follow Christ as his one and only Guide. What joy Peter must have experienced to be that free!

This is the sort of abandonment that I continue to pray for myself and for you. It's a lifelong journey, and just as deeply personal as the relationship Peter shared with Jesus that morning over breakfast on the seashore. It begins with you reaching out and starting a conversation with Him. Tell God that you want Him to be your Guide, and ask Him to place that longing in your heart. If you persevere, you will tap into something that is "infinitely greater"[21] than yourself. You'll get "caught up into the abandonment of God"[22] and the "cheerful compliance with His will."[23] An eternal inner campfire with the Ultimate Outdoorsman.

Questions for reflection and meditation:

Look back and reflect on your answers to the questions that followed the first chapter, except this time envision that God was there with you. He was as present with you in each of those moments as Christ was with His disciples that day on the beach. He enriched your fellowship with one another by His presence and, perhaps, brought you joy.

As you reflect on your answers to those questions, how does the awareness of His presence affect your answers, your emotions, your understanding of His grace?

Prayer:

Dear Jesus, as I sit and reflect on my joy-filled experiences in the wild and the breakfast you prepared and shared that morning with Peter, I weep and yearn. I weep for the joy You placed in my heart, the joy I sense from Your presence in the boat, on a gentle prairie rise, or here alone in my bedroom with You. I yearn for an ever-increasing, deeply personal relationship with my Eternal Trailblazer.

Thank You, Holy Spirit, for bringing me to this place where I want to know and serve You more. It is such a blessing to serve You in even the tiniest way when Spirit-led to do so. Please speak, Lord, and help me to hear You every time. May I never again miss an opportunity or call to work for You! But when I do fail, please guide me back to Your trail with a fullhearted understanding of Your grace and love. For I know that You are "the Father of compassion and the God of all comfort." And I sense you comforting me in all my troubles and leading me to share that same comfort with others (see 2 Corinthians 1:3, 4).

CHAPTER SEVEN

JOURNEY TO PRAYER

Were not our hearts burning within us while He talked with us on the road and opened the Scriptures to us? —Luke 24:32

Oh, how I love to hunt brown bear! The thrill of a spot-and-stalk hunt for dangerous game heightens every sense in my body. I cannot explain it, but it is the way God made me. In my experience, brown bears aren't early risers. They tend to wake mid-morning or mid-day, which makes an early start unnecessary for brown bear hunters. This explains why my "Uncle" Joe and I sat at the table in our Forest Service cabin and journaled our experiences at 9 a.m. while on a five-day hunt on Admiralty Island, Alaska, in May of 2014.

There's a spring steelhead trout run on Admiralty that coincides with the time that the island's brown bears come out of hibernation. Dad and my friend, Dean, were fishing when Joe and I closed our journals around ten o'clock and walked the quarter mile path to the beach, through the Southeast Alaskan rain forest, to see if there was a bear grazing on the tall grass growing in Admiralty Cove. A half hour later, Joe and I sat on a log on the beach, waited, trembled a bit, and quietly prayed that our shots were true.

That morning our prayers focused on our personal safety and that the bear would not suffer. One of the riskier things to do in the wild in North America is to track a wounded brown bear. Neither of us was in a hurry, fearing we might push him deeper into the forest. Funny—as we sat down, we decided that we'd wait a half hour before following-up our shot. But thirty minutes later, we both agreed that the time had passed way too quickly. Why not give it another half hour? (I'm not sure if that was God or our fear speaking—maybe both.)

Usually, though, the time I spend praying outdoors is more restful. God has graced my heart with a sense of wonder and love for His creation. Is it the same for you? If so, it can be overwhelming at times with the thoughts and feelings that flood our soul as we reflect or meditate while alone with Him in nature. Sometimes I have very specific questions for my Father. There are other times when I hear His whisper pressing into my heart, advising me on actions I need to take or not take. I hear God telling me to wait a lot. And praying about these impulses, while out on the boat or in a tree stand, has saved me from more than one mistake. Likewise, I can trace most of my missteps to my failure to seek His guidance in prayer beforehand.

I've kept a field journal of outdoor adventures with friends and family for more than thirty years. They are a personal collection of memories and observations that, on the worst winter days, are a great way to reflect and remember. In a practical sense, they remind me of key details for when I write and submit hunting and fishing articles for publications. I got the idea when I read an account of naturalist John Muir, who referenced his personal field journals.

Over the years, I've also come to appreciate the value of keeping a "field journal" of my daily prayer life. They too help me to reflect and remember. They were my best source for recording many of the thoughts I've shared in this book. The journals, in truth, are just a stack of old note pads in my desk drawer—nothing special. But they are a personal account of how God has intertwined His Word, His Scripture, with my prayer life and day-to-day activities and struggles.

Dietrich Bonhoeffer once said, "If we wish to pray with confidence and gladness, then the words of the Holy Scripture will have to be the solid basis of our prayer."[24] I dumbly stumbled upon this truth—prayer that is not rooted in Scripture is not prayer at all—not long after I decided to try to pray each morning. Simply put, it didn't go well at first. My mind wandered. I struggled to find the words. And when the words did come, they were mostly focused on my wants and desires, and offered little in the form of praise, thanksgiving, or the needs of others. They were inwardly rather than outwardly focused; self-centered rather than Christ-centered; dry words unaffected and uninspired by the Holy Spirit. And I felt this in my soul.

I changed course and began to read a Scripture-based morning devotional. I pulled out my Bible and read the passage that the devotional text cited. After I read the devotional each morning, I reflected and considered how the insights offered in the text related to me and allowed this to guide the direction and perspective of my prayers. In time, I began to underline the Scripture verses and devotional text that spoke to me, and to write my own thoughts in the margins. My prayer life—now rooted in Scripture—began to gain momentum.

I don't remember when this evolved into full-fledged journaling, but that's how it started. I journaled Scripture passages, devotional text, and thoughts that came to me as I reflected and prayed on the words. I began to write down my prayers for the first time, and went back to refine them—days, weeks or months later—as the Holy Spirit brought me insights and greater understanding. There was a gradual yet notable change in my prayers as focus shifted from myself to my relationship with God. The more obedient I was to the wisdom I gained and direction I received during these devotions, the more my morning prayer time grew into a conversation—a daily, intimate conversation with our Father where He responded, in His time, to my questions, requests, and inquiries. I had begun to learn how to meditate and pray.

It is a marvel and a blessing how God speaks to us when we commit ourselves to the conversation and open ourselves to Him. Your heart will burn within you, much like the disciples on the road to Emmaus, as God reveals to you the meaning of the Scriptures and how they apply to your life and situations. Let your journey to prayer begin today!

Questions for reflection and meditation:

In the coming days, I ask that you commit to thirty days of daily prayer—thirty days of exploration. If you don't currently spend time alone with Christ each day, this commitment can change your life forever. No, I'm not exaggerating. If you do have a healthy prayer life, perhaps you just want to change your routine.

In either case, I pray and challenge you to use this book as your Scripture-based devotional for the next thirty days. Don't rush. Set aside thirty to sixty minutes, even if it means getting up earlier for work. Get away from your cell phone and other distractions, and if you're able, bring your field journal with you to your favorite outdoor destination(s) and make time to be alone with God. Maybe it's just a quiet half-hour in your living room in the morning before everyone wakes up.

What is important is that you find a quiet place alone with Christ every day—talk to Him, listen, pray to Him for guidance, and journal your prayers and thoughts. Tell Him what's on your mind, and praise Him for your blessings, no matter how small. Seek His constant companionship and ask that He help you to listen, wait, understand, and accept the journey He has in store for you—a journey like no other.

Prayer:

Good day, Lord Jesus! Today marks a new turn on my journey with You, a milestone of sorts. There's so much going on in my heart and mind and soul that it's difficult for me to get a clear-eyed view of Your reality. Please help me—as I dedicate myself to a prayer life with You—to get out of my own head and show me my heart. And as our conversation grows, please give me the peace and wisdom to sort through my feelings, thoughts, hurts, needs and desires and to sense Your will for my life.

Help me to climb a little higher with You, today and every day forward, Father. It is such an incredible gift to have access to You through prayer. I trust, as we move upward along this trail together, that You will reveal to me more of my heart and Your will. And when those difficult times come, where I must travel though the "valley of the shadow," I have faith that You will lead me safely through the dark and comfort my soul (Psalm 23:4). Please make me "strong, firm and steadfast" for the journey ahead (1 Peter 5:10). For I "know that suffering produces perseverance; perseverance, character; and character, hope." And Your hope never disappoints, because of the love you pour into my heart through the Holy Spirit (Romans 5:3–5).

30 DAYS OF EXPLORATION

DAY ONE

Lord, teach us to pray. —Luke 11:1

Today is an opportunity to renew, refresh, or begin your conversation with God. You may feel uncomfortable or uncertain about this step. Perhaps you're burdened with guilt for having ignored the relationship for some time. For many, there will be joy or excitement over the renewal that the next thirty days will bring to their relationship with Jesus Christ. Can you sense the powerful presence of the Holy Spirit as you close the door to your room and make time to be alone with Him? If you can't just now, I encourage you to stay committed to the process. If you reach out to Him earnestly and faithfully, He will respond.

Now that you're sitting away from all distractions (including your cell phone), how do you begin? Oswald Chambers said that the biblical "idea of prayer is that we get to know God Himself. . . . Be yourself before God and present your problems—the things you know you have come to your wits' end over."[25] This is where your journal entry may help you. Write down the situations that are troubling you, and earnestly ask God to guide you through them. Add the names of loved ones and others you feel led to pray for as you slip deeper into communion with Him.

Journaling your prayers this way will help bring clarity to them as you begin a very personal dialogue with God. You can return to this list each day during your dedicated prayer time to help you fight off distractions and mind wandering that tends to happen to all us. You can also continue to include new names and refine your questions or requests each day, as God provides insight and direction.

This "prayer list" will evolve as you grow in your relationship with Christ. And in time, if you are faithful, obedient, and patient, it will become a list of answered prayers! For now, remember that this is meant to be a heartfelt exchange between you and God, and that He is with you as you trust Him with your most private thoughts. Don't overcomplicate things. It may be as simple as asking Him, "Lord, teach me to pray," and expect that He will.

Prayer:

Dear Lord, I want to know You more. My heart yearns to walk with You. I feel it, but it is so much harder than I thought it would be. Help me, guide me, Jesus, to give over all I have and all I am to You. Please give me words as I pray. And please put people in my life that encourage and push me infinitely toward eternity with You. I praise You with all of my heart and strength, Lord, for Your grace, love, and tender kindness. Amen.

DAY TWO

I saw the Spirit come down from heaven as a dove and remain on Him. —John 1:32

We all experience moments or periods where we question if God is present in our lives. Sometimes this is due to our failure to kindle the relationship with our Savior. In other cases, it is a test—God will test our obedience and faithfulness in the same way a parent entrusts a child with increasing responsibilities.

For me, the most recent experience of this kind of separation happened in the summer of 2017. The three years prior to that, most of my devotions and prayers took place in our living room during the early morning hours before my children awoke. Nested in a bush outside a window was a pair of doves. Whether it was the lights burning brightly beside their nest or a natural occurrence I didn't know of, those doves seemed to wake each morning with me and, as doves do, they would coo from their roost.

Over time, their warm trills became a part of my daily worship. In my heart, the sound of those doves reflected both mourning and joy. And at some point in my journaling, I began to recognize that this mournful, joyful sound was very similar to the way my soul was affected by the Holy Spirit—mournful for my sin and failure to nurture my relationship with Jesus Christ, yet joyful for His saving grace and forgiveness. Their low-pitched song to each other reminded me of the Holy Spirit's presence—a glad, loving burden that compelled me to seek and grow closer to Him.

I began to pray that God would press down on me with the loving burden of His Holy Spirit with greater intensity; that He would guide and push me forward to address the areas in my life that needed to change—obstructions that were preventing me from growing closer to Him. All the while as I prayed, the cooing of those doves somehow heightened my awareness of the presence of His Spirit. Their calm, comforting tones were a blessing to my prayer life.

Then came the summer of 2017, a period of great upheaval for my family—a change in jobs, unforeseen moving expenses, and new schools for our children, just to name a few. My dad was also critically injured in an ATV accident, and all of it seemed to crash into my life at the same time. Financially, spiritually, and emotionally it was an incredible challenge for our family. As a result, I dove deeper into my devotions, praying for strength and God's help. Yet, there were no immediate answers.

For the six weeks before and after our move from Michigan to Florida, I struggled to sense God's presence in our home. On one balmy morning in late July, I found myself asking God, "Where are you?" I knew we would get through this because I had faith He would get us through it. I prayed earnestly that I would just hear from Him—anything. Almost immediately, I got His answer from outside my Florida window—the sound of doves cooing in the distance. Instantly, I felt His Holy Spirit—His joy—wash over me.

It was only later that I would recall John 1:32—"the Spirit came down from heaven as a dove." More recently, I've learned that the Hebrew word for meditation, *hagah* (as in Psalm 19:14), is also the Hebrew word for the cooing of doves (as in Isaiah 59:11).[26] God is truly amazing. He lovingly sent the doves that morning in answer to my prayer.

And as he continues to reveal Himself to me, I know God will certainly show Himself faithful to you. I encourage you to stay strong in your commitment to daily devotions, whether you sense God's presence every time or not. My continued prayer is that God will press down on you with the same loving burden of His Holy Spirit, compelling you to pursue Him with greater intensity and hope.

Prayer:

Jesus, I lift You up this morning. You are the one true Savior. And You desire to build a deep and personal relationship with me. Me? How utterly amazing that You reach across time and space directly into my heart and touch my soul! You inspire me through Your creation, and the more I welcome You into my heart, the more I feel Your Spirit burn within me. I love You, dear Jesus, with all of my heart, soul, mind and strength. Thank You for Your relentless, loving pursuit of me.

DAY THREE

Come, let us go up to the mountain of the Lord, to the temple of the God of Jacob. He will teach us his ways, so that we may walk in his paths.—Micah 4:2

The devil took Him to a very high mountain and showed Him all the kingdoms of the world. —Matthew 4:8

In the fall of 2008, my hunting buddy Gary called me excitedly on a Thursday morning and told me to take Friday off of work. The forecast showed that we were going to get three consecutive clear days—a rarity in Southeast Alaska. The good weather would make it much safer for us to climb and camp for a couple days at higher altitude. We would finally get a chance to pursue the mountain goats that reside in the "archery only" area south of Juneau. We'd spotted goats on these mountains before, but only from sea level, through windows of cloud cover. It was their instinctive "strategy of elevation" among dense clouds that made them a challenge to hunt.

Oswald Chambers once offered the insight that both God and Satan also use a strategy of elevation.[27] What did he mean by that? Well, in the case of evil, every time we give in to a temptation, it becomes that much easier to commit the same sin the next time. It also becomes that much easier to commit the next, more woeful act, as well. In that way our sin is elevated, and we find ourselves on increasingly higher places or pinnacles, where there is poor footing and little room for error without risk of falling.

When God employs the strategy of elevation, He uses the Holy Spirit to show you what you must do to elevate or grow your relationship with Him. Once He has shared this with you, it is your choice to make. The more you obey God's direction, the easier it is to maintain your footing as you climb higher with Him. Instead of clinging to cliff edges emotionally or in your interactions with others, you find it wide open and safe to move.

God-given elevation brings a sense of freedom and peace that rises as we overcome temptation and remain true to the convictions shared by the Holy Spirit. And like our physical bodies, the more we climb spiritually—listening to and obeying Him—the stronger the Holy Spirit grows within us. Lift your sights and make your way up the mountain of the Lord. Strike the path that will continue to elevate your walk with Him.

Prayer:

Help me to rise higher with You, Jesus. I surrender my heart to You and ask that You lead me upward. I accept that it's impossible for me to see beyond the next rise, but I trust that You are here with me guiding my soul and lifting my spirit with Your joy during difficult times. Please give me the strength, courage, and steadfastness to continue this ascent with You each day, my Lord. Now that I'm on this path with You and sense Your presence, I can imagine no other way.

DAY FOUR

Ask and it will be given to you; seek and you will find; knock and the door will be opened to you. —Matthew 7:7

One of the scariest outdoor moments I've ever experienced was as a seventeen-year-old walking to my stand in the morning before daybreak. As I moved cautiously that quiet, cold morning in the dark through a familiar hollow, a bobcat let out a blood-curdling shriek from a very nearby hillside. I was a relatively inexperienced woodsman and had no idea what animal or thing would make that kind of terrifying noise. If anyone had been there to witness it, I'm certain that they would have gotten a good laugh. I was visibly shaken as I continued to walk through the darkness.

With experience I've grown more comfortable moving through the wild in the dark. This progression in my skills and understanding in the wild is very similar to my prayer life. When I first started to try to pray, it felt as though I was sending up balloons in the dark without any confidence of them being heard, much less answered. With experience, I've learned that any prayer offered without the firm belief that God will answer it is hollow and meaningless.

Is this your mindset when you pray? For most of my life it was. To be completely honest, it's still a challenge, mostly because it requires patience and trust. I want God to respond when I want Him to respond. And when He doesn't answer me as quickly as I want Him to, I struggle to maintain trust, to keep faith. I begin to forget His promise, "Ask and it will be given to you."

For many of us, it boils down to our independence as we struggle to surrender our will to God. It requires the kind of faith that Christ intended when He said, "Whoever humbles himself like this child is the greatest in the kingdom of heaven" (Matthew 18:4). It requires each of us to possess the kind of faith in Christ that a beloved child places in a parent or guardian to meet their needs.

One key way for us to demonstrate our faith is waiting patiently and obediently for Him to answer our prayers. The longer we wait on Him in heartfelt submission, the more we properly focus our attention on God rather than our perceived needs and wants.

The more we rely on Him to guide us in His perfect time—not ours—the more our faith in Him will grow. Or as John MacBeath said to those who ask the Lord to guide them, "You may not always see Him, but you can walk by faith in the dark if you know that He sees you, and you can sing as you journey, even through the night."[28] That is faith!

In fact, God always seems to provide us with His answer at the last possible minute to increase our reliance and trust in Him. He is the God of the eleventh hour. Yes, we should all have goals and aspirations, and we should discuss them with God during our daily prayers as we work toward them. But He wants us to become totally dependent on Him during the journey, to pray, to listen, and to wait as He provides course corrections. Focus on Him, and don't worry about the near or distant future. He will open the door if you will only ask, seek, and knock!

Prayer:

Dear Jesus, please help me to reach beyond myself—beyond my limited faith to trust You in complete surrender and peace. So often, I've wrestled with You for control, and it never ends well. I want to learn to walk by faith and not by sight. Teach me. Bolster my shoddy trust and enable me to feel, to sense Your Spirit moving within me and guiding my steps. This is the faith that I want to claim and nurture in my heart, Father.

DAY FIVE

Jesus made no reply, not even to a single charge.
—Matthew 27:14

The largest and most elusive whitetail bucks typically don't grow to their enormous size by making unnecessary noise or running about in ways that put them in danger. They're intentionally cautious with their every step. Funny thing is, the only time that they alter this behavior is when they're in the rut—when they're chasing does during mating season. While humorously similar to mankind, that point will have to be explored another time. What I'd like you to consider is how the whitetail's resolved timidity—an instinct that keeps it alive and enables it to thrive—is so different than the human actions many of us display each day.

We're quick to react aggressively when we sense an accusation or threat. During the most difficult situations—situations where I'm being unfairly blamed—I desperately want my accuser to see things my way, so I rush forward in my response. Rather than displaying a loving submissiveness that would surely de-escalate the tension, I often allow anger, self-pity, or pride to take hold, and I blurt out something to defend myself. It's in that moment, whether I'm guilty or not, that I miss an opportunity to show the love and patience of Christ to my accuser. What happens? It inevitably makes the situation worse.

God does have a sense of progression (a sense of humor as well) about these circumstances. As I've matured in my relationship with Christ, the Holy Spirit has improved my ability to navigate these conditions. But every time I clear one elevation, I find that there's yet another higher mountain for me to ascend. With each new phase of life—work, marriage, children, teenaged children—comes more opportunities to show loving kindness in response to adversity, pain, or anger.

So I ask you, what is your response when you are accused—fairly or unfairly—by the ones you love most? Our culture has turned "submissive" into a bad word, but it isn't. If you submit to the guidance of the Holy Spirit that dwells within you, He will guide you through. You see, there is pure beauty in the way that Christ silently responded to Pilate in Matthew 27:14. Ultimately, He drew His inner peace and joy from God alone, not the opinions of His accusers.

You can do the strong thing by not reacting. By holding your tongue. By keeping the peace.

Prayer:

For many years and in many circumstances, Lord, I've been the rich, young ruler (Matthew 19:20). When I've come to You in prayer, and You so clearly spoke to me of what must be done, I've failed to show the tender heart of submission and surrender to Your will, Your control. But I come to You today, Father, and ask You for a new heart, a heart that rests in You in the face of unfair comments, attacks or injustices. I seek a heart that puts Your will above my own and the gentle nature to endure unfair scrutiny—perhaps from the ones I love most—and love them back. Such grace and submissiveness require Your power and peace to dwell inside of me, Lord Jesus. Only You can do this. Help me, please, to rest in You in every daily encounter and show Your love to others during the most difficult circumstances.

DAY SIX

Bear with each other and forgive whatever grievances you may have against one another. Forgive as the Lord forgave you. —Colossians 3:13

In 1823, Hugh Glass was a member of an expedition that left St. Louis to ascend the Missouri River en route to the Rockies. Hugh had lived with the Pawnees for roughly four years. And while not designated as a leader of the expedition, Hugh was heavily relied upon for his knowledge and experience as a gifted outdoorsman, hunter, and tracker.

That summer, after surviving deadly encounters with natives, Hugh was brutally attacked by a grizzly bear. His body was devastated. He should have died from his wounds. And the men who were ordered to stay with him until he was well enough to travel, Jim Bridger and John Fitzgerald, didn't believe that he would survive. Fearful of dying themselves from the native tribesmen that were seemingly all around them, Bridger and Fitzgerald abandoned Hugh Glass and informed the expedition's leaders that he was dead.

No one can argue that our society loves a revenge story. Our movie theaters and book stores are filled of them. Admittedly, *The Count of Monte Cristo* is a favorite of mine. And if Hugh's account is familiar to you, it's likely due to Leonardo DiCaprio in *The Revenant*, a story that culminates when Hugh Glass hunts down John Fitzgerald to exact revenge. However, that ending is Hollywood fiction. The true story of Hugh Glass's recovery and survival was legendary among frontiersmen.

Yes, he did track down and confront Bridger and Fitzgerald with revengeful intent. But written accounts show that both Fitzgerald and Bridger, perhaps somewhat out of fear, sought Hugh's forgiveness. And while we can't know exactly what was on his heart, Hugh didn't kill either one of them. Instead, he walked away.[29]

What does this tell us about our collective appetite for retaliation? Our personal appetite for retribution? Could you be holding a grudge against a friend, family member, or coworker because they've failed to live up to your expectations? One thing is for sure, embracing those emotions will choke the Spirit that you are now on the journey to finding within yourself. You can't expect people—people with the same sinful and broken nature as you—to meet all your requirements. Only God can fill that void. Forgiveness is the only way to heal your wounds, and that's a good thing.

Is there someone that you need to forgive today, to forgive as the Lord forgave you? If so, commit your resentment to God, and allow Him to heal the bitterness. It's what He does best.

Prayer:

Fill my heart with forgiveness, please, Lord. Seek out my resentments. Help me to identify them and purge them from my heart. Give me the strength and love to show Your grace and mercy to all who have wounded me and to live out this forgiveness every day forward. I desire a true and full heart, Lord, that draws nearer to You every day. And I know this cannot happen if my heart is filled and numbed with unforgiveness toward anyone. Thank you for the grace You've shown me, Father. Please give me a heart, a desire to share Your grace with others.

DAY SEVEN

I will give thanks to you, LORD, with all my heart.
—Psalm 9:1

On the day before Thanksgiving in 1985, I watched the sun rise over West Virginia from a poplar tree in a small hollow near my grandparents' cabin. There was a thin layer of snow on the ground, and the valleys and hillsides were all a bright white in the morning sun. Surrounded by three mountains where my family had lived for almost 200 years, I sat in my stand hoping for a shot at my first buck.

That deer finally arrived around noon, and never has such a small, spike buck been so celebrated. I remember vividly my grandfather's face when Dad and I told him I got a deer. How he proudly drove his tractor to retrieve the young buck for me. Yet, looking back, that's not my favorite memory from that year. Thanksgiving Day holds my favorite recollections of our West Virginia log home.

Eight or ten cousins slept on the floor with a half-dozen aunts and uncles on beds in the single room upstairs. Our grandparents had a small bedroom downstairs. Grandma was always there in the morning to watch her family filter down the stairs. She sat there, contentedly in her favorite chair, reading the Bible as her beloved family awoke and greeted the day. The noise from children, retold hunting stories, and smells from cooking would grow throughout the afternoon in anticipation of our family's Thanksgiving meal.

Homer and Ruth Lemasters were the last of our family to make this property their home. Our shared memories of Elk Fork are still washed in the praise, fellowship, and thanksgiving they shepherded during those family gatherings—gatherings overwhelmed by the presence of the Holy Spirit. Looking back, it was as if our Thanksgiving celebrations were the culmination of a near 200-year family chorus rising up from the mountains and hollows and streams of West Virginia to the heavens in praise and thanks to God.

Yet, even with these robust memories, my family and I regularly fail to give thanks to God with our whole heart. And if we aren't careful, our ungratefulness can grow to become the "gateway" to sins like greed, envy, jealousy, and lust.[30] Or as the disciple Paul said, "For although they knew God, they neither glorified Him as God nor gave thanks to Him, but their thinking became futile and their foolish hearts were darkened" (Romans 1: 21).

Let us all strive to raise our praise to the heavens—not just on Thanksgiving Day, but year 'round—and "give thanks in all circumstances, for this is God's will for you in Christ Jesus" (1 Thessalonians 5: 18). Offer Him simple, heartfelt praise during your morning devotion. Tap into your family's faithful traditions, build on them, and share them with others. If you're among the first of your family or circle of friends to be a follower, start your own humble traditions of giving thanks to God. Let us all join the eternal choir of followers with voices raised in thanks for Christ's loving presence and blessings today!

Prayer:

Today, I give thanks, Lord. I am unworthy of Your love and grace, yet You continue to seek and embrace me. You came to set my soul free, to be my Savior. Praise You, dear Jesus! As I sense Your Presence, my heart swells with a yearning to know You more each day. I love you, Lord. I thank You. And I praise You for the peace, revival, and healing you brought to the world.

DAY EIGHT

Humility comes before honor. —Proverbs 15:33, 18:12

Humility comes before honor. It's so important that God said it twice. As Richard Foster pointed out in *Celebration of Discipline*, "More than any other single way, the grace of humility is worked into our lives through the discipline of service. . . . when we set out on a consciously chosen course of action that accents the good of others and is, for the most part, a hidden work, a deep change occurs in our spirits."[31]

That's a meaty quote. But there are three points there that really deserve attention. First, humility can't be pursued. It is "worked into" our lives—in this case, through self-sacrifice and service. Service is an outward expression of the effect that God is having on your life, your soul. If you are growing in your relationship with Christ, you likely feel compelled to serve. In fact, His Spirit is wasted on us if we only keep it to ourselves.

That's not to say we should just rush out and do something, which is the second point to be made. "Consciously chosen"—we need to take the matter to God in prayer and ask Him where He wants us to serve. "Not my will but yours be done" (Luke 22:42), right? Sadly, more than once, in order to do something, I've committed myself to charities or projects before taking them to God in prayer. The result of my "rushing in" is usually lackluster or average. My failure to seek God's direction—to ask Him where He wants me to serve—winds up hurting the very people that I was there to help.

Foster's point about service circles back to humility—"hidden work." This is increasingly complicated in the world of smart phones and social media. But it speaks directly to how much humility is working itself into our hearts. That's not to say that social media is entirely bad, but it addresses the intent of our posts. Do you post to Facebook, Twitter, or Instagram to raise awareness and involvement with your charity, or so that people will think well of you? Do you post to share experiences, or to seek acceptance and approval? Only you and God know the answers to these questions, and they're certainly worth taking to Him in prayer.

Prayer:

Please, Father, give me a humble heart for serving You. At this point in my life, I am no longer a young, blank canvas. Instead, I am a humbled man whose life canvas is made new and clean by Your grace alone. And now I wait Your brushstrokes, Lord Jesus. Please guide my hands, my soul, and give me patience. Help me to remember the wisdom of Psalm 27:14, "Wait for the Lord; be strong and take heart and wait for the Lord." And as You reveal to me where I am to serve, may I move forward with a humble heart of faith and trust, seeking only Your will.

DAY NINE

He withdrew by boat privately to a solitary place.
—Matthew 14:13

As I wrapped up my devotion this morning, I was once again overwhelmed by how much God wants to be involved in the smallest details of my life. Yet, even though I'm fully aware of this truth, I continue to miss opportunities to take daily matters to Him in prayer.

I've spent a significant sum of money this week (money that my family really can't afford) and committed a lot of time to fixing a truck that I purchased only last month. My greatest disappointment isn't that I bought it. It's that I failed to talk it over with God beforehand. I've had several lively discussions with Him since this purchase of mine.

Pascal once said, "One-half of the ills of life come because men are unwilling to sit down quietly for thirty minutes to think through all the possible consequences of their acts."[32] While true, I don't think Pascal took it far enough. Most of the ills of my life have begun with my failure to take things to God in prayer, then wait and listen for His reply.

God wants to talk with us about our everyday happenings, and we should hand them over to Him—each and every one. Often during morning devotions, He will grant me simple solutions to household repairs, provide ways to engage my teenagers, or give me just the right words for a passage of this book. While these insights are not always deeply spiritual, they speak to just how much God wants to be involved in our lives. It's not difficult to get the conversation started through meditation and prayer. And when you receive a clear answer—moments, days, weeks, months or years later—the full realization of God's presence in your life will strengthen your faith.

Richard Foster wrote that "Christian meditation, very simply, is the ability to hear God's voice and obey His word. It is that simple. . . .

It involves no hidden mysteries, no secret mantras, no mental gymnastics, no esoteric flights into the cosmic consciousness."[33] It can start with a quiet conversation alone in your room where you give the Holy Spirit your full attention as you read a Scripture passage and reflect on how it relates to your daily life. Take your issues to Him in prayer and listen.

As you meditate and pray, has the Spirit shared with you insights and direction about your daily life—something you need to do, or perhaps *stop* doing? Find your solitary place, listen, and obey, and you'll find that He will never stop sending His guidance your way.

Prayer:

As I sit quietly alone with You, Lord, I bring to You my hurts, hang-ups and hopes. I don't want to move forward without clear guidance from You. Please stir my heart, help me to sense Your will, and nudge my soul in the right direction if I'm to move at all. Forgive me for the many times I've acted without coming to You for guidance. I yearn to hear "the still small voice" and then, only then, step out in complete trust and obedience with You. This is the life I want to live. Some would say it's too difficult or a lofty, unrealistic ideal. In truth, dear Jesus, I now understand that it's a free and joyful soul that walks with You in child-like trust.

DAY TEN

Whoever believes in Me . . . out of his heart will flow rivers of living water. —John 7:38

Theodore Roosevelt navigated the River of Doubt after losing the presidential election of 1912. I'm not being philosophical here. Roosevelt co-led an expedition down the Rio da Dúvida, the River of Doubt, in Brazil after his final bid for public office. Only eight years after telling the nation that he would not seek a third term, Roosevelt had abandoned the Republican party and run as a third-party candidate. The loss was an incredible blow; he'd been one of his country's most popular presidents.

Like the true outdoorsman he was, Roosevelt planned an expedition into the unexplored Amazonian River (Now called the Roosevelt River) to help shake off the hangover of the election. In fact, his wife wrote, "I think he feels like Christian in *Pilgrim's Progress* when the bundle fell from his back," in referring to the burden that was lifted from her husband when he refocused his energies from his campaign to the Amazon.[34]

Like you and I, there is little doubt that Roosevelt's greatest struggles and tragedies—e.g. childhood illness, the loss of his first wife, and the death of his youngest son in World War I—significantly shaped his faith. I'm also certain that he drew comfort from God's creation. You see, Roosevelt's adventure into the Amazon jungle, after his failed 1912 campaign, wasn't the first time he found solace in the outdoors. In 1884, after his mother and wife died of different illnesses on the same day, Theodore Roosevelt moved from New York to the wilderness of the Dakota Territory.

From these experiences, Roosevelt emerged to re-marry, raise six children, and become the 26th President of the United States. And it was as President in 1909 that he said that it was his "greatest joy and glory that, occupying a most exalted position in the Nation, I am enabled ... to hold up Christ as the hope and Savior of the world."[35]

Where did he find this strength? Roosevelt answered that question in Medora, North Dakota, in 1903 when he wrote, "It was here that the romance of my life began."[36] It was Roosevelt's wilderness experience that shaped his inner being.

Are there rivers of doubt that are flowing through your life—matters that you need to bring to Christ through prayer? Sometimes we just need to get away to that place outdoors where we feel closest to Him in order to have that conversation. One thing is certain in all of this: if you believe and follow through in your pursuit of Christ, out of your heart will flow rivers of living water instead of doubt. He will guide you through the most troubling situations and, with the benefit of time and understanding, grow your faith in the process.

Prayer:

Dear Lord, I sit before You this morning and reflect on my own wilderness experiences. The hurt, the pain, the loneliness—oh, how the doubt and despair would consume me were it not for You. Instead, I give them to You, Father. And in return, You give me hope. You've shown me the miracle, the ability to feel Your loving joy in the midst of profound sadness. I treasure this time alone with You. Please pull me closer to You when the doubts and fears come and give me the peace and wisdom to fearlessly take the next step with You.

DAY ELEVEN

In all things God works for the good of those who love Him. —Romans 8:28

My father, Roger, is a vibrant, engaging man. And on Sunday morning of the 2017 Memorial Day weekend, at the age of 73, he led my sister's family on a five-mile hike through the mountains surrounding our cabin in West Virginia. He shared stories with four of his grandchildren as he led them to a family cemetery on a nearby peak. He was "in his glory" as he shared his favorite memories with the ones he loved most.

That afternoon as he was enjoying his family, his health, and the activities of such a blessed day, his life was radically altered when his ATV rolled on top of him. Rescuers carefully placed him on a backboard and drove him two miles through the woods to a waiting ambulance. Next, he was transferred into a helicopter that flew him to the West Virginia University Hospital. That evening, doctors strategized how they would best stabilize him and repair his ten broken ribs, six fractured vertebrae, and crushed right hip. It was the most painful experience of his life.

We all thanked God that Dad survived the accident, but how did my father choose to handle it? It was only a few weeks after the accident that he admitted to me, "God's not done with me yet." He refused to wallow in self-pity or anger at God, though he may have expressed anger or desperation in his prayers. But God expects us to do that (Psalm 22 is an example from David). After careful reflection and prayer, Dad concluded that God was going to use this accident for good. The accident led my father to a greater reliance and stronger relationship with his heavenly Father.

Strangely, it's through struggles that most people experience the greatest personal growth. And if you think about it, a life without adversity would be a sad existence. God recognizes this truth and uses it to benefit us and all mankind. The troubles and sacrifices of

Moses, Joseph, and most of all Christ, are all incredible examples of how God takes immeasurable pain and suffering and uses it for the benefit and salvation of His followers.

While none of us would invite hardship, we should be thankful for it. In today's reflection, if you embrace God and seek His strength and wisdom as you endure this life, those challenges will work together for good if only you will reach out and love Him.

Prayer:

Dear Jesus, as I sit at Your feet today, I want to thank You for the understanding, growth and blessings that have poured from the most difficult moments of my life. It was not all that long ago that You confronted me with a clear choice—bitter or better? Thank You for taking my hand. Thank You for taking the worst period of my life and making it also my best. It sounds strange to say, but I would gladly do it again, Father, to experience this life-changing growth with You. A struggle confronted with You at my side, Lord, is a lifelong blessing and opportunity for soulful growth.

DAY TWELVE

You also, like living stones, are being built into a spiritual house. —1 Peter 2:5

There are few moments in my life as profound as the peace and excitement I feel from a deer stand. To sit quietly with anticipation in God's creation, whether perched in Elk Fork, West Virginia in my favorite tree, or on a boulder overlooking a mountain meadow on Douglas Island, Alaska, it brings hope and enthusiasm for what may come.

Such time alone in nature is a beautiful thing. It's an opportunity to reflect, meditate, rest, pray, and play. Yet, when the day ends, we often sense that there is something missing within our soul—fellowship. We're ready to re-gather with friends and family to share our stories and observations from the day, whether it's around a fire at hunt camp or over the dinner table at home. I'm sure you've felt this pull after a day in the wild. The experience, often joyful, shared as you eat, drink, and talk with others, is a gift from God. It's every bit as important to us, and likely more, as the time we spend alone.

This same point is true of our need to worship Christ with other followers, for we are living stones "being built into a spiritual house" of God. And we aren't built to worship Him only by ourselves. After all, when you get alone with the Holy Spirit each day, what are you really asking Him to help you accomplish? Love, serve, forgive, submit? You can't accomplish those things without being regularly, actively involved in a Christ-centered community, which is the church. You can't live out your faith without being in communion with others while serving Him. Or as Josh White of Door of Hope Church says, "You cannot grow as a Christian alone."[37]

As you walk down this pathway with Christ, take time to consider your commitment to worship and fellowship. Do you come together regularly with other followers to praise God and live out your faith? If not, I have no doubt that He has placed that burden on your heart.

Kris Kristofferson expressed this compelling sense so well in his lyrics to "Sunday Mornin' Comin' Down."

> 'Cause there's something in a Sunday
> that makes a body feel alone.[38]

Alone. There's only one way to fully satisfy that feeling deep within you—to fill the void of aloneness and separation from Christ—and that is in communion with other followers of Christ. Commit to gathering in fellowship to praise and worship our Father every week. Allow God to use you as living mortar as He builds His spiritual house here on earth.

Prayer:

Father God, the closer I get to You, the more my heart desires Christ-centered fellowship with other believers. I can't walk this journey alone. Thank You for the brothers and sisters in Christ You've brought to me, Lord. Thank You for the strength and wisdom of Your guiding Spirit as we encourage one another and face our daily challenges and fears. And thank You for the possibility, the hope, of newfound, God-led friendships as well—for with each new kinship one man sharpens another, as "iron sharpens iron" (Proverbs 27:15). Lastly, dear Jesus, when we come together to worship You, may our voices and spirits rise in communion and celebration in a heart-felt chorus that is pleasing to you!

DAY THIRTEEN

When He heard that Lazarus was sick, He stayed where He was two more days. —John 11:6

Have you ever noticed—as a hunter or fisherman—how much time we spend waiting for something to happen? We wait for an outgoing tide or a full moon for the bite to pick up. We wait for that magical hour just before dusk, hoping that the big buck we have on our game camera may show himself before dark. As outdoorsmen we study patterns in nature and through our observations and patience, we try to use them to our advantage.

God is not all that different. He uses waiting to grow our intimacy and dependence on Him. Waiting for the precise moment—and seemingly the last possible minute—He uses time and experience to draw you closer, to strengthen your obedience, hope, and faith. He also uses waiting to increase your understanding and reveal His intent for you and your God-led desires. This is what Jesus did for Mary and Martha. They just wanted their brother, Lazarus, to be well. Jesus waited until He could give them the revelation of eternal life.

Oftentimes our greatest awareness of the power and presence of the Holy Spirit comes after a long-awaited answer to prayer. And when the answer finally comes, it's occurred to me that God didn't just answer my prayers—He perfected them at the exact moment in my life when I was truly ready to receive the blessing. In those moments, the Holy Spirit was so powerful, so present, that my knees buckled, and I was brought to tears.

This was the case after the birth and adoption of our son, Elijah. The sense among the entire family still endures—a sense of being made whole. It was an eight-year journey between the birth of our second and third children, and Elijah's arrival didn't just fill a shared sense of absence in our family. It perfectly completed our family.

Thank God for the powerful effect of His silence. If you feel He is leading you somewhere and you continue to pray, listen, and patiently wait, it will have a remarkable impact on your relationship with Him. Have hope that God will answer you. He's merely using this time in your life to draw you ever closer to His side. Double your efforts to stay true and to praise Him. Have faith and trust that He will answer you in His time and in the most glorious way!

Prayer:

Lord, the year that lies ahead of me is seemingly full of unanswered questions. Last night You left me with the words "Blessed is he who waits" (Daniel 12:12) as I went to bed. And this morning as I rise to read this devotion and write this prayer, I'm confronted, once again, with the need to show You trust and patience. The words for the devotional came so easily months ago. But it's so hard, harder than I thought it would be. You know my prayer list, Lord, and You know my needs better than I do. And I must admit, the more I've grown to trust You, the more the future holds an unknowing excitement for where You will lead me. I lay down my life, Jesus. You know my heart. Please give me the strength and wisdom and understanding to wait and move out with You alone.

DAY FOURTEEN

Let the sea resound, and everything in it, the world and all who live in it. Let the rivers clap their hands, let the mountains sing together for joy. —Psalm 98:7, 8

When conservationist John Muir explored the Tracy Arm fjord in 1880, he traveled in a dugout canoe with Tlingit guides. His description of the icy inlet, published in *Travels in Alaska*, is still among my favorites. Referring to Tracy Arm as "the wild, unfinished Yosemite," Muir went on to write that "the drainage of fifty [glaciers] or more pours into this fjord. . . . The water spaces between the bergs were as smooth as glass, reflecting the unclouded sky, and doubling the ravishing beauty of the bergs as the sunlight streamed through their innumerable angles in rainbow colors."[39]

Situated about forty-five miles south of Juneau, Tracy Arm is among the first places my wife and I visited when we moved to Alaska. Traveling up the narrow thirty-plus-mile inlet, we were overwhelmed by the jade-colored water and the sheer rock walls rising close to four thousand feet on either side of us. Though it was August, we passed through miles of dense icebergs and fast-moving current and marveled at mountain goats standing on distant cliff faces. Bald eagles, seals, and gray-and-white-feathered terns with their jet-black heads were seemingly everywhere, often perched on the icebergs that fell from the calving North and South Sawyer Glaciers situated at the head of Tracy Arm.

We were extremely blessed with clear skies that day, a rare occurrence in Southeast Alaska. And with the aid of that sunshine, we caught a glimpse of what Muir witnessed in 1880—sunlight streaming off of snow, dazzling blue water, and majestic icebergs. Incredible! He said it best about this "hidden Yosemite"—a "grander array of rocks and waterfalls I have never yet beheld in Alaska."[40]

"Let the sea resound, and everything in it, the world and all who live in it. Let the rivers clap their hands, let the mountains sing together for joy." This is a Psalm that heralds "the coming of Christ"[41] with joyful praise. It's a chorus that has been sung since the dawn of creation in Tracy Arm—long before Muir arrived—and it continues to this day. Praise God for such beauty and the joy of nature He placed deep within our soul. It's in those moments when we are stirred that we sense all creation celebrating our Maker.

Prayer:

Praise You, Lord, for the beauty of Your creation and the promise of a new day. Take all that is behind me and use it for what is ahead. Pour me out as a blessing to others. Strengthen my heart with the song of the mountains as they "sing together for joy" and the rivers as they "clap their hands" (Psalm 98:8). Bring my spirit back to You each morning in daily surrender, Father, and send me out into the world with a joy-filled, tender heart of service for You.

DAY FIFTEEN

Let us keep in step with the Spirit. —Galatians 5:25

Prayer is hard. It can be boring. It is often a struggle to find the words. And for me, there are definitely times when prayer is a labor of love—heavy on the labor. Have these thoughts crossed your mind in the last fifteen days? Have they affected your dedication? If so, what you're experiencing is completely normal. I've heard similar thoughts preached twice this week by two different ministers. God must be trying to tell us something as we reach this midway point in our thirty days of prayer.

Truth is, it's easier to have your kids play video games than to play outside with them. It's easier to watch that next football game than to do something loving for your spouse. It's easier to watch television than read a book. And it's definitely easier to sleep in or satisfy some other distraction than to follow through on your prayer life. "The spirit is willing, but the body is weak" (Matthew 26:41). Never a truer word!

But prayer is also powerful, and the adversary knows this. As the veteran devil Screwtape told his nephew Wormwood in C.S. Lewis's *The Screwtape Letters*, "The best thing, where it is possible, is to keep the patient from the serious intention of praying altogether. . . . Whenever there is prayer, there is danger of [God's] own immediate action."[42] This is no surprise to us. Communication is essential to every relationship, and our relationship with Christ is no different.

If you've reached this fifteenth day of devotion, your daily conversation with God and your prayer list is likely growing. If you've missed a day here or there, you've also probably sensed the void or experienced the impact of failing to take time alone with Him. This feeling gives you a little insight on the difference between a life led in full devotion to Christ and life as an out-of-step Christian. The longer the time spent between our conversations with God, the more half-hearted, lukewarm, and frustrated our faith becomes.

It's clear that the best way to keep in step with our eternal Guide is through a dedicated prayer life. Pray for the strength and fortitude to stick with it. Seek Christ's love and sense His presence in your daily prayers and devotions. Watch how He stirs your soul and changes how you interact with others as the Spirit increasingly influences you in everyday life. This takes unmistakable discipline for sure, but it's always better to push through and climb higher—to strive for a lifelong conversation with God through prayer.

Prayer:

Lord, I start my prayer time this morning asking You to show me my heart. Too many times in my life I've allowed unhealthy pursuits (and even healthy pursuits, for that matter) to consume me, and in the process, I failed to tenderly love those closest to me. I failed to draw pleasure from the simplest exchanges with my children and others. And I failed to spend time with You alone in prayer. Please reveal to me, dear Jesus, any pursuit that consumes me to the detriment of those around me or my relationship with You. Help me to surrender it to You entirely. Thank You for life's simple pleasures, Lord, and please help me to hold them in a proper perspective.

DAY SIXTEEN

Keep asking that the God of our Lord Jesus Christ . . . give you the Spirit of wisdom and revelation, so that you may know Him better. —Ephesians 1:17

There's a great tradition on the Chesapeake Bay that I took for granted as a boy. It's the habit of Virginians and Marylanders of referring to fishermen, oystermen, crabbers—men and women that work on the water—as "Watermen." And, as we discussed in chapter two, we outdoorsmen should find comfort in the fact that Jesus chose four watermen to serve as His disciples. After all, these were men that shared our love, respect, and fear for the wonder, beauty, and power of His creation. They sensed God's presence in nature and responded to His call.

As our faith and prayer life grows, we should cherish this connection with Christ and His first four disciples. You are a waterman. Draw comfort, respond, and persevere with the understanding that—just like you and me—these watermen made mistakes and sinned as well. "Keep asking" for "the Spirit of wisdom and revelation, so that you may know Him better." And as Peter experienced that morning with Christ after their "breakfast on the seashore," praise God for His loving nature, patience, and forgiveness.

This is the sort of abandonment that I would pray for you. It is a difficult yet joyful lifelong voyage that is just as personal as the relationship Peter—the waterman disciple—shared with Christ that morning over the meal He cooked for them. It begins and ends with you reaching out and conversing with God—simple, heartfelt prayer. The God of infinite grace will guide you if you persevere and maintain the course.

Prayer:

For so much of my life, Lord Jesus, "clouds and thick darkness" (Psalm 97:2) surrounded much of You and Your Word. With a spirit of disobe-

dience and rebelliousness, I plowed forward, trying to somehow contain You or restrict You to only parts of my life. But as I reflect and pray this morning about a Savior that would lovingly, tenderly cook breakfast on the seashore for a friend that had recently betrayed Him, my heart swells. Thank You for bringing the conditions that led me to abandon my life to You. And thank You for Your faithfulness, that the more I lay down my life and seek You, the more You lift the "clouds and thick darkness" surrounding You and Your Word, and reveal to me the heart of my Savior.

DAY SEVENTEEN

Present yourself to Me there on top of the mountain.
—Exodus 34:2

When I was nine or ten years old, my dad and I loaded our gear into our old K5 Blazer after a day of fishing on the mill pond near our home. Dad worked two jobs in those days, which included teaching night school, so I cherished this quality time with him—as any young son would. I wanted to be useful and show him that I could help him unload the boat, so I shuttled the net, tackle box, paddle, and life jackets up the hill to the truck from the old johnboat we kept there.

Dad carefully loaded the rods. And when he wasn't looking, I "helped" by rolling up the rear window onto the rods that were sticking out. His rod tips broke and, even at that age, I knew immediately that Dad would have to work even more time at his second job to replace them.

What did he say when he rounded the corner of the truck to discover my mistake? "That's all right, buddy pal. It'll be okay." It was the kind of calm, loving grace in a moment of surprise that, especially as a father, I marvel at today. That's what my dad is like—calm, loving, and gracious.

How do you think God would describe Himself if you asked Him what He is like? Almighty, Lord of lords, Maker of all heaven and earth? We get a clear answer to this question in Exodus 34 when God proclaims to Moses that He is "the Lord, the compassionate and gracious God, slow to anger, abounding in love and faithfulness, maintaining love to thousands, and forgiving wickedness, rebellion and sin." Wow! It's the only place in the Bible—at least that I'm aware of—where God answers this question so directly.

As you contemplate this amazing truth—that your eternal Guide is a God of compassion, love, faithfulness, and forgiveness—how is your relationship with Him affecting your ability to show His grace to others? From strangers you meet on the street, to your closest loved ones, are you granting them the same grace that God has so freely granted you? As Josh White shares in his sermon on Psalm 139, "Grace is not grace if it doesn't change anything."[43]

Yes, God's grace, with our willing efforts, will get us to the top of the mountain—whatever mountain gets in your way. He knows you'll make mistakes, but He also knows what is in your heart, and He'll help you achieve the highest level of compassion, love, faithfulness, and forgiveness if you truly seek Him. With determination, patience, and most of all the power of the Holy Spirit, God will help you to press on and climb higher!

Prayer:

Dear Lord Jesus, please give me a heart filled with Your grace. As I seek and walk with You, please press deep within my soul Your compassion, love, faithfulness, and forgiveness. We can't manufacture opportunities to show grace, Father. They arrive in Your time, often when we least expect them. Give me a heart that so dwells with You that when the moment arrives—instead of giving way to anger, frustration, or hurt—I show Your tender, loving kindness. Your grace and mercy have changed my life, Lord. Please help me to share it with others, that they may know You better.

DAY EIGHTEEN

The Spirit Himself bears witness with our spirit.
—Romans 8:16

Have you ever tried to guide someone on a hunt, fishing trip, or some other outdoor pursuit? It's not easy. You're responsible for every detail—from what to eat, to the must-have gear. And it all has to be planned out and packed up before you ever take your first step on the trail, make a cast, or take a shot. Once the adventure begins, the unplanned obstacles and challenges that arise will test even the most experienced guides.

On May 11th of 2014, I led such an expedition—a black bear hunt in Southeast Alaska—with my father and friends, Dean and Joe. Our hunting party was on the third day of a five-day hunt, and no one had pulled a trigger. We had stalked nine different bears, but due to miscommunication, largely on my part, Dad and Joe had passed on shots of worthy bears. I began to feel the pressure. After all, these were my closest friends and family, and I wanted them to succeed. More than once, I succumbed to the pressure and said things to my father that I later had to apologize for. I certainly didn't show him the grace that he had so often shown me.

As we rounded a point in our skiff on the afternoon of our third day, I prayed to God for peace and guidance. I gave up control of the situation to Him and focused on simply doing my part. I felt the tension decrease and hope increase as Joe located a bear grazing on the shoreline a mile or so ahead of us. A typical Southeast Alaskan drizzle continued to fall, so I wiped my binoculars as Dad brought the skiff to idle to check our wind. We picked a rocky outcropping where we could beach our boat and take a closer look without being discovered. Ten minutes later, our decision was clear—this was our bear. What followed was the best and most improbable hunt of my life.

If it's difficult to guide a person in the wild for a few days, it's next to impossible to be their guide in life. There's only one Being that can fill that role. We're called to share our journeys to faith and to teach (i.e., disciple). It's God's job to do the supernatural part—to reach out to a person, speak to them in a very personal way, and save their soul. Yes, parents may guide their children on some level for a while, but every Christian parent eventually prays that their child seeks Christ as their ultimate Friend and Guide.

We're summoned to "Go therefore, and teach [disciple] all nations" (Matthew 28:19). We're also called to love one another. "As I have loved you, so you must love one another" (John 13:34). After that, we're simply meant to trust the truth that we sense in our heart—that "when a man will listen, God speaks."[44]

Let the Holy Spirit—mankind's eternal Trailblazer—bear witness with your spirit and guide them the rest of the way.

Prayer:

Lord Jesus, as I look over my prayer list this morning at all the names, it would be easy to grow overwhelmed. From loved ones and friends I've known most of my life to recent acquaintances, I have many requests. Yet, only You truly know their needs and possess the power to meet them. So, I humbly ask You, Father, please lead me in prayer and bring my people—the names You've placed on my heart—Your revival, healing, reconciliation, and peace. I turn them over to You, surrender any anxiousness, and trust that You will guide them the rest of the way.

DAY NINETEEN

Where can I go from Your Spirit? Where can I flee from Your presence? —Psalm 139:7

The closer we grow to our Father, the less coincidence there is in our lives. His hands are everywhere, involved in the smallest detail. And the more we talk with Him, the more we see and attribute to Him.

In 1912, Ruth Kathryn Fiber was born in a small shack on an oil patch in the mountains of West Virginia east of the Ohio Valley. There were roughly a dozen homes in this meadow. The men worked for the oil company. Their children played in the stream and on the hills that circled their homes. And like so many other small enclaves around the country, the residents gave their community a proper name—Pollard. This one even had a post office.

The residents led a humble life. The roof on Ruth's shack was made of tin, and in the winter when the fire in the stove waned overnight, condensation and ice would coat the inside of the tin ceiling. Ruth's mom and dad strung cheesecloth above their heads to catch the water that dripped down when they stoked the cook stove in the morning. Her mother cooked in a cast iron skillet that her ancestors brought with them from Germany. My father still has that skillet—seems only proper, since Ruth was my dad's mother.

While vacationing with my wife in Rocky Mountain National Park in Colorado in 1998, I decided to explore a used bookstore after several days of hiking. As I searched the many shelves in utter glee, I found a book printed in 1899 called *Daughter of the Elm: A Story of the West Virginia Hills*. It was well-worn, and someone had sketched a tree inside the cover. I read enough to suspect that it was about the region of West Virginia where my family hailed. I bought the book, intending to give it to my dad for Christmas.

I forgot about the book that year, so it was Christmas of 1999 before Dad received it. He devoured it and confirmed that it was a story about life in northwestern West Virginia before the Civil War. He even shared it with Grandmother Ruth when she came to visit that spring.

Ruth possessed a very child-like simplicity, but she was getting old. And when she opened the front cover of the book and saw Gertrude's name, she began to talk of Gertrude as though she knew her. My dad corrected Ruth and let her know that I'd bought the book in Colorado. That it was a new find and not a long-held family heirloom. Ruth then said that the tree sketched in the front cover seemed familiar. Dad let her go on to pacify her. Then, there in the back of the book Ruth found a postcard—a postcard both Dad and I had missed. It was addressed to Gertrude Reppard in Pollard, West Virginia.

Please understand, Ruth was a constant storyteller. We rarely drove by the cow pasture along Pollard Road when I was a child without Ruth reminding us that it was where she was born. And like many children who've heard a story repeatedly, I didn't truly appreciate what that pasture represented to Ruth. I simply dismissed or ignored her. Now, suddenly, with the arrival of this book from Colorado, Pollard came to life for me. Gertrude was Ruth's next-door neighbor in Pollard. She made Ruth's first doll baby and also gave Ruth's family their pet dog.

That book was nothing short of a gift from God! I once thought, what a marvelous coincidence. Of course, now I recognize it for what it was—a small yet heavenly miracle, evidence that God cares about the tiniest details of our lives. Once we recognize and believe it, this new perspective strengthens our faith to know that He is present and involved in every moment of every day.

He's with us now—me as I type, you as you read—reaching out to both of us. There isn't anywhere you can go to escape God's presence or His love. Nowhere.

Prayer:

As I sit before You this morning, Lord, and reflect, I am confronted with my lack of faith. With the benefit of time, I look back and see countless details—always at just the right moment—that You introduced and shaped circumstances to pour blessings into my life. Yet, I come to You this morning mulling over my concerns for family, career and finances. I believe, Lord Jesus, and trust You with all of my heart, soul, mind, and strength. "Please help me in my unbelief" (Mark 9:24). I trust that You love and care for the well-being of my family infinitely more that I.

DAY TWENTY

Whoever loses his life for me will find it. —Matthew 16:25

Most outdoorsmen love wilderness adventure and survival stories. I am constantly on the lookout for true accounts of men and women that exceed the boundaries of what the civilized world believes can be endured and survived in nature. The Author and writers of the Bible share this passion of ours. From David living in caves to the nation of Israel wandering in the desert, to Christ being tempted after forty days in the wilderness without food—God must love a good survival story, because the Bible is full of them!

Interestingly, in every one of these biblical accounts, whether an individual or an entire nation, success is determined by the subject's willingness to surrender their will to God. It's when they willingly accept their situation and look to God for direction that they thrive in the most difficult circumstances.

And the same could be said for us. Until we surrender our will to God, we are merely surviving day-to-day. Surrender, listen and obey—and there's a freedom that overtakes us, a sense of peace and love that stays with us through the most difficult situations because we rest our faith in Him.

Are you struggling to surrender your will to God? It's no wonder. We all do. Oswald Chambers said of this matter that "the great crisis [in life] is the surrender of the will."[45] But if God is to truly be your Guide, it must be done, for it is our independence—our "deliberate and emphatic independence of God"—that is the source of our sin.[46]

And what happens when you finally take this most difficult step? You find that surrender is only the beginning! From the point of submission going forward, God patiently and thoroughly—one time after another—begins to point out your sins and the aspects of your life that you put ahead of Him. Each time you listen and obey His guidance, you take a step closer to Him. When you fail, He is patient, but it is unlikely that He will give you a new "assignment" until you complete the current one.

From this experience, we learn that surrender is not as simple as giving up control. It is a decision. You take a hard look at your priorities and decide to be obedient to God, putting Him ahead of everything else in your life. He's not going to do it for you, but He will strengthen you through the presence of the Holy Spirit. He does it by convicting you to seek Him more and more, or as Chambers puts it, "The whole of the life after surrender is an aspiration for unbroken communion with God."[47]

Like Elijah's survival story at Kerith Creek (1 Kings 17), God is not satisfied until we rely entirely on Him. It's counterintuitive, but if you lose your life in order to find His greater purpose, you'll experience the greatest freedom you have ever known.

Prayer:

Good morning, Lord! Today, as I seek to grow closer to You, I ask You to search my heart, soul and mind. Show me where I am failing to surrender. I want nothing between us, but I can't do it on my own. I need Your Spirit, Your power to help me act according to Your good purpose (Philippians 2:13). I desire this intimate relationship and friendship with You with all of my being, Father, that I may serve You in this life and the one to come.

DAY TWENTY-ONE

God made Him who had no sin to be sin for us.
—2 Corinthians 5:21

Have you ever gone on an outdoor adventure—seemingly planned and executed perfectly—and have it not work out as you had intended? I think we all have. Hunters, fishermen, explorers, or climbers, it doesn't matter. We've all had those days where we did everything we were supposed to do, but the weather, equipment, game, currents, or terrain just didn't cooperate. Sometimes even our companions slow our outings down to a crawl or derail them completely.

Strangely, for me it's this same unpredictability that also makes hunting, fishing, and hiking my favorite pastimes. (That's why we call it hunting and fishing, and not shooting and catching!) It's the intrigue and unknown challenges that bring passion and thrills to our outdoor adventures. The parts that are out of our control—the unplanned and unanticipated—that keep us coming back and bring us joy.

The same thing could be said about our relationship with God. It's not our simple faith and obedience that gets us "right" with Him. There's a supernatural part that is out of our control. Yes, we have a critical role to play in believing and obeying, but it was Jesus who truly set things right. We could do everything perfectly after we come to know Christ, and there would still be an infinite canyon between us and God were it not for one thing—the Son of God died for us. He didn't do it simply out of love and empathy. He did it to atone for mankind's broken nature.

It was only through Jesus Christ's willingness to obey the Father—to bear the burden of our sins through His death and resurrection—that we are set free from them. It's the part that is out of our control, the supernatural part that allows us to experience our ultimate joy. Our spiritual DNA is grounded in Christ. We were each created through Him, therefore it was necessary for Him to take away our darkness by becoming darkness in those last moments on the cross. How painful and yet how powerful that Someone so flawless would be willing to become what He despised the most. Still, the lovely irony remains—He became sin to make us clean.

Prayer:

Dear Jesus, as I bow my head and close my eyes this morning, I picture myself sitting silently, restfully at Your feet. In Your presence, I feel entirely loved. You know me completely and, even at my worst, You love and care for me as Your son. It's a love founded on Your willingness to sacrifice Your life to free me. It's a never-ending love, that in Your defeat of death You offer me the promise of eternal life with You. That kind of love goes far beyond my understanding, Lord. It brings me joy, and it carries me forward. Please dwell so deeply within me, that in my daily interactions, Your amazing love overflows from me.

DAY TWENTY-TWO

He leads me beside quiet waters. —Psalm 23:2

Richard J. Foster once wrote, "In contemporary society our Adversary majors in three things: noise, hurry, and crowds."[48] I'm sure these words come as no surprise to you. Anyone who's spent time around a campfire with friends, sat quietly by themselves on a bluff glassing for game animals, or enjoyed the morning hours fishing or paddling over calm waters, has sensed this truth. Yet, our world continues to accelerate.

The 24-hour news cycle, smart phones, and social media are all ingrained components of our society. They fill our lives with information and busyness. Work schedules, social commitments, family, traffic, crowds—they're inescapable at times. And if we allow it, the devil will use them to consume us, leaving no time for the Lord in our life. Or as Carl Jung put it, "Hurry is not of the devil; it is the devil."[49]

This, of course, begs the question: Are you the source of "confident calmness"[50] in your workspace, family and church, or are you so frayed from constant activity that it hurts your ability to listen to and interact with others? Where are those quiet waters God promises? As we ask ourselves this question, we should remember that the verse that precedes this promise is "The Lord is my shepherd." If He's your *Shepherd*, of course, this makes you a *sheep*—one that is to receive the promise of "still waters." You can only find this peace when you surrender your will and entrust your every need to your heavenly Shepherd.

It is a God-given irony that through your faithful devotion and surrender to God—an act that much of mankind associates with weakness—that the Lord will "make you strong, firm, and steadfast" (1 Peter 5:10). You become the voice of "strong, calm sanity"[51] in your workspace, family, church, and community as you grow more intimate with Him! You attain a "mature manhood, to the measure of the stature of the fullness of Christ" (Ephesians 4:13) when you accept Him as your Shepherd.

Prayer:

O Lord, this morning I come to You with a spirit struggling to sit still, surrender, and sense Your presence. I know this time alone with You is essential to my daily walk, yet my heart grows anxious with life's unknowns. Even as I try to focus on You intently and write this prayer, the busy demands of the morning ahead creep into my mind. Help me to rest in You now and throughout the day. Don't let the crowds, traffic, work, bills, and myriad of other stressors overtake the peace You give so freely. I give this day entirely to You, Father, come what may, and lead me forward with a spirit intent on walking calmly through it all with You.

DAY TWENTY-THREE

For a little while you may have had to suffer grief in all kinds of trials. These have come so that your faith . . . may be proved genuine and may result in praise, glory and honor when Jesus Christ is revealed in you.
—1 Peter 1:6-7

When I was a second grader at Achilles Elementary School, one of my friends in first grade told a bully on the playground that I would fight him. Some friend, right? But I allowed myself to get pulled into the fight, and it didn't end well—for me. As for my "friend," at least he knew that he couldn't make it alone. He sought help from someone stronger, as we all should. So, please consider this for a moment—when a crisis comes, who do you bring to the fight?

We all have someone or something in our life that gets us worked-up or angry. It's easy to fall into a pattern of distress, defensiveness, and viewing everything from our own (usually selfish or threatened) perspective. All the while, Christ is waiting there, ready to change our point of view when the test comes. We don't have to react like an angry bass on the end of a set hook every time we're hurt or threatened. Don't take the devil's bait! Instead, calmly, quietly bring Christ to the fight.

If you're in a committed relationship with Jesus, you can draw strength from the Holy Spirit during these situations. You can climb higher and view things from Christ's patient perspective—unrushed, calm, and confident. Say a quick prayer in moments of irritation and ask for His guidance. Maybe just lovingly excuse yourself and walk away to gather your thoughts until it's clear what God would have you do. Much like Christ when the crowds, noise, and commotion began to wear on Him, step away for a moment of communion with the One who has an ocean of patience at your disposal.

This kind of tolerance is honed best by God's moment-by-moment presence. It takes time, and it's a choice. You can choose to contribute to the explosion of emotion, or you can strive to walk in the love of Jesus Christ. It's easy to take the bait impulsively when something surprises you. But it's just as easy to speak God's truth to the situation if we are "slow to speak and slow to anger" (James 1:19).

For a little while you may suffer grief in all kinds of trials, yet your faith will be proven genuine as you exercise the supernatural strength that is available through Jesus Christ. I don't believe any of us can withstand life's strains and struggles without it. And the good news is, we don't have to!

Prayer:

Lord, as I come to You this morning and reflect on my yesterday, all that I can say is, "I did it again." I took the bait and allowed my anger to get the best of me. Instead of calmly, quietly bringing You to the fight, I allowed ongoing mistakes by my bank and health insurance to raise my anger. Rather than surrendering the situations to You, I charged in on my own. You know my heart, Lord. Thank You for showing me this is an area that needs work. Please give me the Spirit-led self-awareness and strength to be "slow to speak and slow to anger" (James 1:9). Help me, please, Father, to exude a firm but loving presence in the midst of life's frustrations and hurts. This is only possible by looking at these situations through Your eyes.

DAY TWENTY-FOUR

Since the creation of the world God's invisible qualities—His eternal power and divine nature—have been clearly seen. —Romans 1:20

In November of 2002, my wife, Kim, and I drove with our ten-month-old daughter, Catherine, across Tennessee late one evening on our way to join family in Arkansas for Thanksgiving. Still an hour or two from our hotel, our truck broke down and left us stranded on a dark, silent highway with temperatures below freezing. Thank God we had a cell phone connection, and in a half-hour our tow truck arrived. What followed? You could make a Hallmark movie from the acts of kindness that cascaded through our lives those next three days.

Our tow truck driver immediately recognized that Kim was cold and shaking, so he drove my wife and baby girl to a hotel ten or so miles up the road while I stayed with the truck. Later, as I spoke with Kim in our hotel room, she was transformed as she shared how the loving lady at the front desk offered to reduce our room charges by two-thirds when she learned of our circumstances. I was a bit overwhelmed myself as I explained to Kim that our tow driver's friend had offered to fix our vehicle in the hotel parking lot the next day.

The following morning, our mechanic drove me in his old pick-up to get the part we needed from a friend of his. When I asked the cost of the part, the man smiled and said, "I'll take eight dollars." The truck was fixed by dinnertime, and Kim and I marveled at the loving way so many people came to our rescue. But our engine problems weren't over. Soon after we got on the freeway the next day, the truck began to sputter from an entirely new problem. We made our way to a nearby dealership wondering what to expect next.

Given the long line outside the service center, we might have been there for another day or two. But as I explained our circumstances to the man at the service desk, he said, "I've heard of you from a friend of mine at church. I'll put my best guy on it, and we'll see if we can get you out of here soon." In less than an hour, at almost no expense, our family was back on the road. Simply miraculous! Once again, God used our troubles to remind Kim and me of our many blessings and thanksgivings.

Let me ask you: Has God put people in your life that, through acts of kindness, revealed the love of Christ? This is not a coincidence. You're witnessing God's invisible qualities at work. But more importantly, He's also using you in order to show kindness to others. When He places you in situations where you feel guided to help someone, that's God! By maintaining a conversation with God that enables you to clearly hear Him, He is achieving miracles through you by the power of the Holy Spirit. He will call upon you more and more if you keep the conversation going.

Prayer:

Lord, what a morning! For so much of my life, I worked and maneuvered to pursue my goals without any consultation with You. I obsessed over details and outcomes and diligently attempted to engineer circumstances as if I was in control. But today—with a heartfelt desire for obedience and surrender—I thank You for my successes and failures. With the benefit of time, I see the doors You closed and opened. And I recognize the amazing men and women of God You placed in my life to help lead my hardened, controlling heart to You. Thank You, Jesus! I am truly blessed. In that same sense, Lord, I pray that You will use me in the lives of other souls who are finding their way to You. Help me to look at each encounter through Your eyes, listen intently, and share Your Word.

DAY TWENTY-FIVE

Speaking the truth in love, we will in all things grow up into Him. —Ephesians 4:15

Perhaps the greatest good ever shown to us is the willingness of others to share their faith and speak the truth in love. God is a maestro at moving people around—seemingly out of nowhere—to precisely where they're needed the most. That's how He works, through friends, family, neighbors, strangers—anyone that speaks the language of love. Just as my grandfather shared the gospel and—in full awareness of my sin—lovingly led me to Christ. He understood the power, and sometimes the discomfort, at the mention of the name of Jesus. This was the moment I accepted Christ as my Savior, and it started with a faithful follower speaking the truth in nonjudgmental love.

The simplest encounters can be watershed moments for a soul that has strayed or is searching to know God. It begins with a single follower reaching out. That means *you*, extending yourself when you feel God prompting you to speak to someone, share your faith, or offer a prayer. This is when an ordinary moment becomes extraordinary—when you obey God and open the door for the Holy Spirit to work in someone's life.

Sadly, so many of these encounters never happen due to our own shame, fear, or busy schedules. We deny the Spirit the opportunity to work in a person's life because it's uncomfortable or inconvenient. This problem continues as many of us—including myself—spend years or even decades never moving past this point in our walk. We're content to stay believers rather than faithful followers. We sit idle rather than climbing higher.

Truth is, Christ should so rule our lives that we act on His behalf without even knowing it. We should be blind to the fact that we are sharing the goodness of God with everyone we meet. That's the peak that we're climbing for, and it will take everything we have to reach its summit. Or as the Reverend Terry Fullam once said, "It doesn't take much of a man to be a disciple of Christ, but it does take all of him."[52]

Shine God's brilliant light where the enemy hides in shadows. Open up to hearing the truth in love as well as speaking it. They're both important milestones on the path as you seek in grow up into Him.

Prayer:

There's a line in one of my son's favorite songs, Lord: "It's harder than I thought it'd be. It's taking every part of me."[53] It's a thought that's echoed through my head for some time now as I mull over old choices and their fallout. These are choices that, while I've seen tremendous healing, also had incredible bearing on the person I am. And as I reflect on that thought this morning, Lord Jesus, it's as if—through my journaling and prayer—you are having me "spell out my soul."[54] In showing me my heart this way, Father, I feel simultaneous joy and a healthy discontentment. I pray that feeling never leaves me, that a joyful discontent forever compels me forward to seek You and share Your Word.

DAY TWENTY-SIX

And who knows but that you have come . . . for such a time as this? —Esther 4:14

For anyone involved in an ongoing conversation with God, there is likely something—big or small—that He is asking them to do. It's why William Sloan Coffin said that "the leap of faith is a leap of action rather than a leap of thought."[55] It's why Mordecai pleaded with Esther to take action by reminding her that she likely came to her royal position with the king "for such a time as this."

On Sunday, February 7, 2016, I woke up to this kind of struggle. My wife and children were in Florida, and I had committed to Kim, myself, and most importantly God, to begin work on this book while they were away. It was the third day without them and I hadn't started yet, and overwhelming doubt consumed me. *Who am I to write a book? What do I really have to offer?* It's especially heartbreaking to doubt an inner passion. That really hurts!

To avoid this conversation with God, I skipped my morning devotions and reluctantly went to church. The sermon began as I slumped into my seat in the last row. You can see where this is going, right? God spoke clearly and directly that morning through Pastor Jason's message.

As he preached "for such a time as this," he continued, "you are in a position of responsibility. If you've been entrusted with the gospel, if the truth of who Jesus is, what He's done, and why it matters has taken root in your heart, then you have a responsibility to let that truth permeate the world around you."

He went on, "Standing up is not always easy, and I hope that we can come to a place as believers where we don't look at actions as heroic, but simply as being obedient. Doing what we have all been called to do."[56] Ouch!

Big or small, your act of faithfulness to God's direction will bring you to a fuller, more complete relationship with Him. It doesn't matter if anyone ever reads this book. The faithful act of submission to His direction is what matters. It's through our "leap of action" that we learn more about God's ways as well as ourselves. How about you? Are you being faithful to His request?

Oswald Chambers once wrote that we should "never allow a truth of God [that has made its way home to our] soul to pass without acting on it."[57] That's such a beautiful image, and one that we could all do more of. Write the truth in your prayer journal then turn it into action. Find comfort and joy in the act of faithful obedience and, more importantly, rely on the power of the Holy Spirit to do it. While you're at it, get ready for your next assignment, 'cause God is not done with you yet!

Prayer:

Good morning, Lord Jesus! Today I call on You for courage and a Spirit-led, all-consuming energy to pursue the actions You place on my heart. Truth is, it's easy to write these thoughts we share in the morning in my journal. The real doubts and fears arrive when I reach the point of action. Grant me, Lord, the calm, trusting wisdom to discern what You want me to do. Help me to know when to wait for additional direction or doors to open. And please, Father, give me the unrelenting desire, faith, and courage to pursue every task, big or small, that You share with me.

DAY TWENTY-SEVEN

The unfading beauty of a gentle and quiet spirit . . . is of great worth in God's sight. —1 Peter 3:4

On the Tuesday after Thanksgiving 2017, I returned to hunt camp for lunch after spending the entire morning in a deer stand. Hungry and eager to hear everyone's morning hunt stories, it took me a while to recognize the wreckage in the yard around the cabin. Trash and a bag of charcoal were spread on the hillside. Deer feed bags were opened, and an entire bag was missing. And why was the ice from my cooler ripped open and lying next to the porch? More importantly, where was the deer that was hanging in the pole barn? The answer was in the bear claw marks carved in the lid of my cooler.

Dad, Dean, Joe and I have shared a lot of laughs about Elk Fork's newest resident. I understand the bear's need for food, but what was it thinking when it opened and spread bags of ice and charcoal? Then it hit me—how often am I guilty of spreading "bags" of harsh and unloving words around my house? I come home from work and traffic and, if I'm only thinking of myself, there's no gentleness to my comments. The people I love most suffer and hurt when I allow self-centeredness to consume me.

We all, I pray, have a person in our life that has demonstrated to us the true gentleness of Christ. Mine was from the hills of Tennessee. She had a way about her—a Spirit-filled, soulful presence—that commanded your attention without ever demanding it. My grandmother's humble, loving, gentle nature gave strength and reassurance to everyone around her, but most of all to my grandpa. Despite all of the strength that he outwardly exuded, she was in many (if not most) ways, stronger than him. And all of this originated from her complete faith in Jesus Christ.

There is unfading beauty in my grandmother's Christ-centered gentleness. And, like joy, you can't seek it or simply decide to have a gentle spirit. It's an outcome. The only way to radiate Christ's gentle Spirit is to love Him "with all your heart and with all your soul and with all your strength and with all your mind; and, love your neighbor as yourself" (Luke 10:27). Allow Him to be your Guide entirely, and your soul will grow a little gentler each and every day.

Prayer:

Holy Spirit, as You continue to re-engineer my heart, please grant me the gentleness that grows from an abandoned, obedient spirit (Galatians 5:23). Remove from me the hard edges, sharp words and forceful nature and replace them with Your understanding, patience and love. Bring all of Your power to bear on altering my disposition and grant me a clear-eyed ability to see things as they truly are, rather than selfishly distorting them. And with this Spirit-led vision, Father, please lead me to pray and discern and act in a gentle, Christ-like way.

DAY TWENTY-EIGHT

Be clear minded and self-controlled so that you can pray. —1 Peter 4:7

In the fall of 2007, my friend Gary and I flew from Juneau to Yakutat, which is a small community near Icy Bay, Alaska. From Yakutat we hired a bush pilot to transport us to a Forest Service cabin near the Alsek River where we planned to hunt for moose. While flying over miles of Alaskan forest and muskeg (marshes), I was struck with how the terrain surrounding our cabin looked incredibly open from the air. Yet, once we landed, even the marshes were difficult to navigate. Visibility was extremely limited, but Gary had done the "homework" for this hunt and remained confident in his plan.

The next morning, we put on our waders and rain gear, and used the canoe kept at the cabin to paddle up a nearby stream made deeper by a series of beaver dams. We occasionally carried our canoe and packs between pockets of water, and after roughly two miles, we arrived at a spot where Gary announced, "We'll have to walk the rest of the way."

Walk? More like slog. We broke a thin layer of ice that morning as we waded through thigh-deep water, forest, and marsh for the next quarter-mile. I wondered where Gary was taking us. Visibility continued to shrink as we pressed deeper into the rugged landscape before he announced, "We're here!"

At that moment, "here" didn't seem too spectacular. We could only see two or three yards ahead, and the woods were thick with large bushes—roughly six to eight feet high. I watched curiously as Gary pushed his way through a line of thick brush. We began to climb. In his preparation for the hunt, Gary learned of a small mound in the middle of a large muskeg valley that rose roughly two hundred feet in the air. And in just a few minutes, we climbed above the marsh and thick shrubs to gaze over several square miles of territory that lay between us and the nearest mountain range. Our perspective had entirely changed.

How similar this story is to our lives! Many of us slog through our daily existence, refusing to exercise the Christ-centered, self-control available to us. Instead, we cling desperately to an unhealthy desire to maintain control over day-to-day life. Even after we come to know Christ as our Savior and understand fully that there is greater freedom in Him, we often refuse to engage that faith muscle, and we remain stuck.

When we could be stronger in Him, we choose to be weaker in ourselves. Is that a guy thing, or what? Yet all we have to do to escape the quagmire and change our perspective is climb higher with Him. Make the effort, and the clear-minded self-control He so willingly offers is yours to be claimed!

Prayer:

Lord Jesus, for the last week or so I've meditated and prayed about the fruit of the Spirit—love, joy, peace, patience, kindness, goodness, faithfulness and gentleness. Today I arrive at self-control (Galatians 5:22–23). In a worldly sense, I've exercised "self" control for most of my life. Ultimately, my internal drive to control my life and others around me brought me to my knees here with You. While painful, I would do it all over again if that's what it took to finally bring my heart to the point of surrender. Thank You, Father, for this understanding and Your grace. Today, all I ask is that You guide my every step and give me the Spirit-led self-control to follow where You lead.

DAY TWENTY-NINE

The greatest of these is love. —1 Corinthians 13:13

If you haven't noticed, you've spent the last eight days exploring the different components of the fruit of the Spirit—love, joy, peace, patience, kindness, goodness, faithfulness, gentleness, and self-control. And while it's listed first in Galatians 5:22 and 23, I saved love for last, perhaps because it's the greatest, or maybe because it's the part of the fruit that gives me the greatest difficulty.

Of course, it is only when we pursue a relationship with Christ that we show increasing portions of His love to others. We also feel a greater sense of guilt for our unloving moments. As the Apostle Paul put it, the closer you move toward Him, the more you "grasp how wide and long and high and deep is the love of Christ, and know this love that surpasses knowledge—that you may be filled to the measure of the fullness of God" (Ephesians 3:14–19). To be filled with the fullness of God is to be so overcome by the Holy Spirit that—consciously and unconsciously—you can't help but share Christ's love with others. It pours out of you.

Christ's love for us is the greatest type of love. Beyond the love of simple pleasures (e.g., food or the outdoors), beyond the love for a human being (who inevitably expects something in return), Christ's love is entirely self-sacrificing. It's the foundation of our faith in God. Without His love, there would be no cross. And without the cross, there would be no forgiveness for mankind. The atonement that we receive through Christ's obedient, self-giving act—His death and resurrection—would be lost. That's the kind of self-sacrificing love we're talking about. The kind that changed the course of history and redeemed all of us.

Remember that faith, hope, and love are eternal, and the greatest of these is love. Nothing and no one can take it from you. Not "trouble or hardship or persecution or famine or nakedness or danger or sword . . . neither death nor life, neither angels nor demons, neither present nor the future, nor any powers, neither height nor depth, nor anything else in all creation, will be able to separate us from the love of God that is in Christ Jesus our Lord" (Romans 8: 35, 38, 39). It's this kind of love that Christ calls us to share with the world. And if you seek Him with all of your heart, soul, strength, and mind, it will change you and your world forever.

Prayer:

Your love is overwhelming, dear Jesus. My words can't capture it, and I am entirely unworthy of it. Yet You give Your love so freely. Please pierce my heart with Your love, Father, that I never again forget, underestimate, or take for granted the love You showed me on the cross. Work Your love so deeply into my soul that I feel barren and hollow without it. And when I fail to show Your love to another, please give me the keen awareness, understanding, and humility to quickly make amends. Praise You, Lord Jesus, for profoundly altering my heart, saving my soul, and giving me the promise of eternity with You. Such love!

DAY THIRTY

Always pray and not give up. —Luke 18:1

You have arrived at the thirtieth day of this devotional, so it seems fitting to talk about hope today—hope for your way ahead. There is great power in the hope that is founded on our eternal Guide and Father. "Against all hope, Abraham in hope believed" (Romans 4:18). Yet, so many of us live in the past and, in some sense, live off of our memories. If we aren't careful, we can find ourselves satisfied with fond memories but fail to strive for our current and future goals. It happens very easily, especially where our relationship with Christ is concerned.

Truth is, if we aren't striving for a deeper relationship with Christ, we are backsliding. If we are living off our memories and past experiences of the Holy Spirit, we are growing further apart from Him. It is hope—hope founded on a strong faith in God—that leads us to climb higher and strive for greater closeness with Jesus. Yes, "our memories are strong, but hope is stronger."[58]

Sir Ernest Shackleton understood the power of hope when he and his crew watched their ship, *Endurance*, break apart and slip under the icy waters of the Weddell Sea on November 21, 1915. The Endurance Expedition had departed Buenos Aires the previous year with the intent of being the first craft to cross the continent of Antarctica. Now, stranded alone on pack-ice a mile from the shores of Antarctica, there was seemingly no hope of survival. Yet, it was in the face of this desperate circumstance that the ship's doctor, Alexander Macklin, observed Shackleton's "real greatness" as a leader. He wrote, "He did not . . . show . . . the slightest sign of disappointment. He told us simply and calmly that we would have to spend the winter in the pack."[59] Shackleton offered his men hope.

Soon after, Shackleton wrote in his journal, "Our hopes were now centered on Elephant Island, which lay 100 miles almost due north."[60] His men completed the daunting trip and suffered through the winter, consuming the last of their rations and what little food they could collect. Many nights were spent "getting what little warmth they could from the soaking sleeping bags and each other's bodies." Still, they kept up hope.

On the morning of April 24, 1916, Shackleton and five other members of the expedition set sail on what many believe to be the most miraculous sea voyage ever recorded. The men sailed roughly eight hundred miles across the stormy sub-Antarctic ocean on a twenty-foot boat that was converted to a sailboat by the ship's carpenter in an attempt to reach a whaling station on South Georgia Island. Conditions during the voyage were miserable, each man battling frostbite. But under Shackleton's leadership and Captain Worsley's keen navigation, the small crew kept up hope. I have little doubt that many prayers were lifted up along the journey.

Upon reaching South Georgia, two men—Worsley and Crean—were fit enough to join Shackleton over the miles of mountainous terrain and glaciers that towered between them and the whaling station. On August 30, 1916, the twenty-two members of the expedition at Elephant Island watched as the "mist opened and revealed the ship for which they had been waiting and longing and hoping."[61] Every member of the expedition survived.

Sometime later, Shackleton would record the following entry in his field journal.

"When I look back on those days, I have no doubt that Providence guided us, not only across those snowfields, but across the storm-white sea that separated Elephant Island from our landing-place on South Georgia. I know that during that long and racking march of thirty-six hours over the unnamed mountains and glaciers of South Georgia, it seemed to me often that we were four, not three. I said nothing to my companions on the point, but afterwards Worsley said to me, 'Boss, I had a curious feeling on the march that there was another Person with us.' Crean confessed to the same idea. One feels the 'dearth of human words, the roughness of mortal speech' in trying to describe things intangible, but a record of our journeys would be incomplete without a reference to a subject very near to our hearts."[62]

Like Peter, Shackleton and the crew of his small boat were met at the seashore (John 21:4) by a holy Guide who quite literally conducted them around the challenging terrain of South Georgia—a coastline that had never before been traversed by man.

And like them, you have completed your passage—these thirty days of devotion. I encourage you to continue onward with your journey of daily prayer. Strive with holy ambition to climb higher and grow closer to your eternal Guide, Father, and Friend. The relationship is just as intimate as Peter's breakfast on the seashore and Shackleton's difficult trek along South Georgia. God so much wants to know you more. You have felt His love and sensed the need to seek Him. Now, always pray and do not give up your faith, love, and hope in Him.

Prayer:

Thank You for these thirty days of prayer with You, dear Jesus. What a journey it's been! As I reflect this morning on the disciples' three-year trek with You leading up to Your crucifixion, I sense a connection with them in my heart—as outdoorsmen, as men struggling with their faith, as followers of Jesus, hoping against all hope.

The deep sense of fellowship I feel with men that would choose to spend a night on the water fishing together (John 21:3), as they search for their next steps, brings a surge of peace and understanding to my heart. I've spent enough time in boats with my closest friends and family—especially when we "caught nothing"—to smile about the questions and conversations I know they shared that night. What would each of them do next? Where would they go? How were each of them handling the incredible uncertainty? Oh, the stories about You they must've retold and rekindled that night!

And shortly after these brothers-in-Christ watched the sun rise over the Sea of Galilee, You met them by the seashore and cooked breakfast for them over a campfire. What a Savior! What a Savior that would allow me to share my memories and hopes with my closest friends through the night—all in the beauty of Your creation—and then lovingly greet me in the morning for breakfast. It makes my heart sing, Father. It makes me certain of Your presence and call every time I've ever experienced the joy of Your creation. And it gives me hope.

Thank You, Lord. Thank You for these thirty days. Thank You for Your friendship. I am excited to share the journey ahead with You.

AFTERWORD

If you continue in My word, you are truly My disciples; and you will know the truth, and the truth will make you free. —John 8:31, 32 (NRSV)

I should probably close with an apology. You see, this book should come with a warning label because I firmly believe in my heart that anyone who asks God to be their Guide, God will pursue that request without fail. If you seek Him and ask Him to help you surrender your will to Him, He will do it! And while you'll experience joy, peace, and grace in the process, it will also be a struggle as the Holy Spirit brings you to a fuller understanding of what it means to follow Christ. If you're patient with yourself and dedicated to following your eternal Guide, your life will become "one great romance, a glorious opportunity for seeing marvelous things all the time," so eloquently put by Oswald Chambers.[63]

Victor Hugo described the journey this way as he grew older and his body began to break down. "Within my soul I feel evidence of my future life. . . . People say the soul is nothing but the effect of our bodily power at work. If that were true, then why is my soul becoming brighter as my body begins to fail? Winter may be filling my head, but an eternal Spring rises from my heart . . . and the closer I come to the end of my journey, the more clearly I hear immortal symphonies of eternal worlds inviting me to come. It is awe-inspiring yet profoundly simple."[64]

No matter where you are on your journey with our eternal Guide, I pray that this book, through your prayers, reflections, and journaling, has brought you a little closer to Him. If these were the first thirty consecutive days that you have ever diligently prayed to God, I reckon that you will sense that something is missing if you suddenly stop setting aside time each day to be alone with Christ.

If so, like Sheldon Vanauken, you have come to understand the truth revealed in Galatians 4:9: "Now that you know God—or rather are known by God—how [can you turn back]?" Your soul will never again be satisfied with the status quo. Continue in His Word to abide more and more in Him as you climb upward toward your heavenly home.

God wants to complete us. He has a target in mind, and we simply can't get there without putting Him first in our lives. God bless.

ENDNOTES

1 Kris Kristofferson, "Why Me" (song), from the album *Jesus Was a Capricorn* (Nashville, TN: F. Foster, 1972).

2 Oswald Chambers, *My Utmost for His Highest* (Grand Rapids, MI: Barbour, 1963), Feb. 15 devotional reading.

3 Lettie B. Cowman, *Streams in the Desert* (Grand Rapids, MI: Zondervan, 1997), 443.

4 Henri Nouwen, *Making All Things New* (New York: HarperCollins, 1981), as quoted in Richard J. Foster and James Bryan Smith, eds., *Devotional Classics* (New York: HarperCollins, 2005), 81.

5 Lettie B. Cowman, *Springs in the Valley* (Grand Rapids, MI: Zondervan, 2016), 61.

6 C. S. Lewis, *Surprised by Joy* (New York: Houghton Mifflin Harcourt [Mariner Books ed.], 2012), 168.

7 Brother Lawrence, *The Practice of the Presence of God* (New Kensington, PA: Whitaker House. 1982), 32.

8 Brother Lawrence, *The Practice of the Presence of God*, as quoted in http://www.goodreads.com/work/quotes/2133549-the-practice-of-the-presence-of-god?page=1 (2017).

9 Josh White, "Boldness from the Spirit" (audio sermon), Door of Hope Church, Portland, OR. Retrieved from http://www.doorofhopepdx.org/wp-content/uploads/2017/09/Boldness-from-the-Spirit.mp3 (January 21, 2018).

10 Chambers, Feb. 19 devotional reading.

11 Editors of *Christian History Magazine*, "Brother Lawrence: Practitioner of God's Presence," retrieved from http://www.christianitytoday.com/history/people/innertravelers/brother-lawrence.html (October 1, 2000).

12 Cowman, *Streams in the Desert*, 138.

13 Lewis, 169.

14 Lewis, 170.

15 Chambers, Feb. 19 devotional reading.

16 Sheldon Vanauken, *A Severe Mercy* (New York: Harper & Row, 1987), 73.

17 "Leap of Faith" (Wikipedia article), https://en.wikipedia.org/wiki/Leap_of_faith (January 29, 2017).

18 Chambers, May 8 devotional reading.

19 Cowman, *Streams in the Desert*, 384.

20 Chambers, Nov. 16 devotional reading.

21 Chambers, Mar. 13 devotional reading.

22 Chambers, Mar. 13 devotional reading.

23 Cowman, *Streams in the Desert*, 113.

24 Dietrich Bonhoeffer, *Psalms: The Prayer Book of the Bible* (Minneapolis: Augsburg Fortress, 1970), 11–12.

25 Chambers, Aug. 28 devotional reading.

26 Walter C. Kaiser, Jr., "What is Biblical Meditation?" from John Woodbridge, ed., *Renewing Your Mind in a Secular World* (Chicago: Moody Press, 1985), chapter 3. Retrieved from http://www.cslewisinstitute.org/webfm_send/860 (September 23, 2017).

27 Chambers, Mar. 27 devotional reading.

28 Cowman, *Springs in the Valley*, 292.

29 Bruce Bradley, *Hugh Glass* (Coral Springs, FL: Llumina Press. 2007), 206, 213.

30 David Whitten, sermon, Fishhawk Fellowship Church. Retrieved from http://www.fishhawkfc.org/sermon/unthankful-the-gateway-sin-sat (November 4, 2017).

31 Richard J. Foster, *Celebration of Discipline* (New York: HarperCollins, 1978 [revised ed.]), 130.

32 Cowman, *Springs in the Valley*, 297.

33 Foster, 17.

34 Catherine Millard, *The River of Doubt: Theodore Roosevelt's Darkest Journey* (New York: Broadway Books, 2005), 47.

35 Theodore Roosevelt, as quoted in William Judson Hampton, *Our Presidents and Their Mothers* (Boston: Cornhill Publishing Co., 1922), 210.

36 Michael F Blake, *The Cowboy President* (Guilford, CT: Rowman & Littlefield, 2018), 251.

37 Josh White, "The Four Pillars" (audio sermon series), Door of Hope Church, Portland, OR. Retrieved from https://www.doorofhopepdx.org/sermons/the-four-pillars/ (September 3, 2017).

38 Kris Kristofferson, "Sunday Mornin' Comin' Down" (song), lyrics © Sony/ATV Music Publishing LLC. Used with permission.

39 John Muir, *Travels in Alaska* (Boston and New York: Houghton Mifflin, 1915), 275, 281.

40 Muir, 270, 271.

41 Matthew Henry, *The Bethany Parallel Commentary on the Old Testament* (Minneapolis: Bethany House, 1985), 1125.

42 C. S. Lewis, *The Screwtape Letters* (New York: Simon & Schuster, 1996), 28, 29.

43 Josh White, "Praying through Grace" (audio sermon). Retrieved October 2017 from http://www.doorofhopepdx.org/sermons/psalms/ (July 28, 2013).

44 Cowman, *Springs in the Valley*, 334.

45 Chambers, Sept. 13 devotional reading.

46 Chambers, Oct. 7 devotional reading.

47 Chambers, Sept. 13 devotional reading.

48 Foster, 15.

49 Foster, 15.

50 Cowman, *Streams in the Desert*, 69.

51 Chambers, Jan. 7 devotional reading.

52 Everett L. Fullam, "The Holy Spirit, the Scriptures, and You" (audio sermon, n.d.). Available from https://lifeonwings.org/library.php (recording #930311-28).

53 Garcia, Glover and McKeehan. Love Feels Like [Recorded by T. Mac]. On This is Not a Test. Franklin, TN: Garcia and McKeehan. 2015.

54 Chambers, Jan. 12 devotional reading.

55 William Sloane Coffin, *The Collected Sermons of William Sloane Coffin: The Riverside Years, Volume 2* (Louisville, KY: Westminster/John Knox Press, 2008), 113.

56 Jason Coplen, "Esther, Week 5" (sermon). Retrieved November 2017, from http://www.crosspointechristianchurch.org/media/media-item/123/02-07-2016-esther-week-5 (February 7, 2016).

57 Chambers, Nov. 4 devotional reading.

58 Roy G. Pollina, various sermons at St. Michael's Episcopal Church, Mandeville, LA, 1996 to 2000.

59 *Shackleton's Antarctic Adventure*, IMAX, 40 min. WGBH Educational Foundation, Boston, 2001.

60 Ernest Shackleton, *South: The Endurance Expedition* (New York: Penguin, 1999), 127.

61 Shackleton, 262.

62 Shackleton, 230.

63 Chambers, May 8 devotional reading.

64 Cowman. *Streams in the Desert*, 216.

ABOUT THE AUTHOR

Scott Lemasters is a thirty-three-year veteran of the U.S. Coast Guard. Born in West Virginia, Scott grew up on the Chesapeake Bay in rural Mathews County, Virginia. He has enjoyed tours of duty in Alaska, Louisiana, Virginia, Maryland, Kentucky, Michigan, and Florida. Of course, this has also allowed for plenty of hunting and fishing opportunities!

Scott's love for fishing began early in life with his father. Together, they have enjoyed rich waters all over the world. From tiger fish on the Zambezi River, to red salmon on Kodiak Island, to walleye on the Great Lakes, Scott offers a wealth of experiences to share. He is also blessed to have pursued a wide variety of big-game animals with "do-it-yourself" hunts for Dall sheep, coastal brown bear, moose, mountain goat, black bear, and whitetail deer. Included in his many adventures are guided hunts for Cape buffalo, sable, kudu, mule deer, aoudad, and mountain lion. One of his proudest outdoor moments was guiding his dad for coastal brown bear on Admiralty Island, Alaska. That said, watching all three of his children—Catherine, Sarah and Elijah—catch their first fish is a very close second.

Scott enjoys sharing hunt stories and the gospel. To contact him about speaking at your church retreat, game dinner, banquet, or other ministry opportunities, you can reach him at LetTheLordBeYourGuide@gmail.com.

TRAILBLAZER MINISTRIES

A ministry dedicated to outdoorsmen and their relationship with our Eternal Trailblazer, Jesus Christ.

True outdoorsmen are inspired by nature. We share an emotional connection to creation that, whether we recognize it or not, is a call from God. Have you responded to this call by spending time alone with Him each day in prayer? If not, you are missing out on His very best for you and your family.

Trailblazer Ministries' mission is to lead outdoorsmen into a deeper relationship with Jesus through daily prayer and fellowship with our brothers in Christ.

You are blessed with a Savior who loves you, cares about every detail of your life, and wants a personal relationship with you. He also enjoys the company of outdoorsmen and sharing a good campfire with his friends—check out the 21st chapter of John!

Visit or contact us at:

TrailblazerMinistries.com

LettheLordBeYourGuide@gmail.com

Please reach out to Scott at Trailblazer Ministries if you'd like him to join or lead your men's ministry event. An outdoorsman's connection to God's creation is a powerful way to share the Gospel and lead men to Christ. And it's entertaining! From funny and captivating hunting and fishing stories to personal accounts of surrender and intimacy with the Holy Spirit, Scott will pray and work with you to pursue the Lord's will for your church retreat, game dinner, banquet, or other event.